P9-BHS-669

ANDY,

WHY DID YOU
HAVE TO GO?

ANDY,

WHY DID YOU

HAVE TO GO?

A MOTHER'S INTIMATE REFLECTIONS
ON THE LIFE AND SUICIDE OF A SON

ANDY,

WHY DID YOU
HAVE TO GO?

A MOTHER'S INTIMATE REFLECTIONS
ON THE LIFE AND SUICIDE OF A SON

Joyce Gatson

Ralph Tanner Associates, Inc.

PRESCOTT, ARIZONA

Blithe Spirit

He had a beautiful smile,

An infectious laugh.

To know him was to love him.

He asked so little, and gave so much.

Why did he have to go, we'll never know.

He is our blithe spirit, forever with us.

We miss him so, but in our hearts we know,

He is resting in God's arms forevermore.

Mom

Andrew Banning Gatson
1973-1994

*"Because the tragedy is not God's will,
we need not feel hurt or betrayed by God…"*

<u>*When Bad Things Happen to Good People*</u>
Harold Kushner

Preface

I don't think I should have to convince anyone that suicide is a serious public health problem. Not only that, but it is reaching epidemic proportions in some groups. Suicide is the eighth leading cause of death in the U.S. In recent years Americans have been very concerned about the number of homicides being committed across the country, but it surprises most people to learn that for every two homicides that take place in the U.S., there are three suicides committed. And suicides and homicides are often related, as was the case in Littleton, Colorado.

Consider youth suicide:

- Suicide is the 2nd leading cause of death among college students.
- Suicide is the 3rd leading cause of death among all those 15-24 years old.
- Suicide is the 4th leading cause of death among all those 10-14 years old.
- The suicide rate for white males (15-24) has tripled since 1950 while for white females (15-24) it has more than doubled.
- The suicide rate for children (10-14) has more than doubled

over the last 15 years.

- The suicide rate for young black males (15-24) has risen by 2/3 in only the past 15 years.
- Adolescent males commit suicide more than adolescent females by a ratio of 5:1.

Characteristics of youth at risk for suicide:

Mental illness - 90% of adolescent suicide victims have at least one diagnosable, active psychiatric illness at the time of death—most often depression, substance abuse, and conduct disorders. Only 33-55% of suicide victims were identified by their doctors as having a mental illness at the time of their death, and only 15% were in treatment at the time of death.

The Surgeon General's Call to Action to Prevent Suicide is the product of an effort that has brought the best science together with the best experience on the subject of suicide prevention. Recently, we held a conference in Reno with researchers, clinicians, survivors and advocates to lay the foundation for a national suicide prevention strategy. Since then, we have been working hard to achieve this goal. There were more than 80 recommendations put forward at that conference.

In the course of reviewing those recommendations, we quickly realized that they could be refined or reduced to 15 essential major recommendations which, if implemented promptly, would greatly help to reduce the number of suicides as well as suicidal behavior. Given that the country is facing an average of nearly 85 suicides and about 2,000 attempts per day, we felt that it was important that we get these recommendations to the public as soon as possible, while continuing to work on a more comprehensive national strategy.

The 15 recommendations revolve around three principles

—Awareness, Intervention, and Methodology—whose first letters form the word "AIM."

AWARENESS

We must promote public awareness that suicides are preventable. We must enhance resources in communities for suicide prevention programs and mental and substance abuse disorder assessment and treatment. And we must reduce the stigma associated with mental illness that keeps many people from seeking the help that could save their lives. The problem of depression, for example, is common in this country and throughout the world. Don't be afraid or ashamed to seek help so that you can continue to be a productive person, or to refer a friend or loved one you believe to be at risk.

INTERVENTION

We must complete our work with public and private partners on a National Strategy for Suicide Prevention. We must eliminate barriers in public and private insurance programs for provision of quality mental and substance abuse disorder treatments. We must institute training about suicide risk assessment, treatment, management and aftercare for all health, mental health, substance abuse and human service professionals—including clergy, teachers, correctional workers, and social workers.

We need to develop and implement effective training programs for family members of those at risk and for natural community helpers on how to recognize, respond to, and refer people who show signs of suicide risk. Far too many health professions are failing to ask about depression or to encourage patients to talk about it. In fact, about 70 percent of elderly suicide victims have seen a health care professional within the month preceding their suicide.

METHODOLOGY

We need to enhance research to understand risk and protective factors related to suicide, their interaction, and their effects on suicide and suicidal behaviors. And we need to increase research on effective suicide prevention programs, clinical treatments for suicidal individuals and culture-specific interventions.

It is my hope that communities, policymakers, civic organizations and individuals will take these recommendations to heart and work to implement them. We must remember that prevention begins at home, and the work of suicide prevention must be done at the community level.

Compounding the tragedy of loss of life, suicide evokes complicated and uncomfortable reactions in most of us. Too often, we blame the victim and stigmatize the surviving family and friends. These reactions add to the survivors' burden of hurt, intensify their isolation, and shroud suicide in secrecy.

Unfortunately, secrecy and silence diminish the accuracy and amount of information about persons who have completed suicide—significant information that might help prevent other suicides.

David Satcher, M.D.
U.S. Surgeon General
May 2000

Foreword

Juvenile suicide is an end result of symptoms that occur earlier. Suicide is the culmination of problems that have come to a head. The juvenile court system does not focus on suicide, but does focus on mental health. Detention officers circulate among the juveniles and report if there is a suicide potential. If it is determined that there is a mental health issue, the court can send the juvenile to a facility for a 24 hour evaluation and get a report from the doctor. The court can also have the juvenile held for 72 hours and the court can order a complete psychological evaluation. This evaluation can be completed before trial or after the juvenile is in detention. Suicide does not occur in a vacuum. The court can schedule counseling for the family and order personal counseling and medical treatment for the child. The court can also order and force parents, if necessary, to follow recommended procedures necessary to help their child.

Family and friends of the juvenile must be a squeaky wheel. Families must push, advocate and fight for the needs of their children. All the people involved with the child's life must advocate for them and perform whatever acts that will benefit that child.

Once a child comes into the court system parents need to not hide the issues but must tell the court what is going on with their child. The squeaky wheel will always get oiled. If parents don't tell the court what is going on with their child the court will never know what problems the child is having. If the parents are not completely honest with the court, no positive recommendations can be ordered to aid the child, and, always, without intervention, there are tragic results.

Parents, neighbors and family members of the troubled child can help the court by keeping the court apprised of developments that are going on in the home or school. Often parents are reluctant to tell the courts what kind of behavior problems the child is having. The ultimate goal of the court is to treat the child up front so the child can grow up to be a healthy productive adult. It doesn't help if the family says everything is fine, and the child is acting out and getting into trouble at school or home. Teamwork and cooperation between the family and court can move mountains to help the children grow out of their problems. Parents, neighbors and family members need to think of the court as a resource that can help.

When we as a public, think of the juvenile justice system we need to put out of our mind all the media images and hype. Do not demonize the court, or the children. The best way to resolve the child's problems is to work in a reasonable manner with them. Our understanding is a quiet gift that may pay results in the future. Look at these children as our own children, not as those children. Look at them as our future parents, doctors, lawyers, business people.

Wouldn't it be better to consider what they might accomplish with our help and guidance? If we treat our children better, they will turn out better. As the adults, we must be positive role models. Children are always watching the adults in their life. As adults, we must respect the children, nurture them, and keep them mentally healthy. Most kids that come through the system are good kids, they simply made a mistake of youth. Eighty percent of the kids who come through the court system and receive a consequence, never come back. Half of the remaining 20 percent are simply curfew problems, leaving only 10 percent that are tougher nuts to crack. So, we must be respectful of them as individuals. And stay involved with them, know what they are doing, where they are, who their friends are and set boundaries. Adolescents need even more supervision and monitoring than younger children, and they need to know adults care about their well-being and futures.

In the court system, experience has taught us that as parents, family and friends, our combined efforts on behalf of the child always improves the situation. Parents can tell the courts the histories of their children, whether one of success or failure, so that we can learn what is positive and what needs to be improved. Parents can lobby the funders, community, community groups and schools for programs to make a difference in the lives of children—funders are tired of hearing from the court, but they never tire of hearing from voters.

The Honorable Maurice Portley
Presiding Judge of the
Maricopa County Juvenile Court
May 2000

"Therefore we pray to You instead, O God,
For strength, determination, and willpower,
To do instead of just pray,
To become instead of merely to wish."

<u>*Likrat Shabbat*</u>
Jack Riemer

Introduction

I have never thought of myself as a writer. The ability to put what I think and feel in writing about Andy's death had only been a wish. However, after many hours of reflection, and effort, this manuscript has become a reality. This manuscript is written for my benefit, although my hope is that by sharing my pain other families with similar experiences may be helped in some measure by this book. If these reflections help just one person other than myself, the excruciating pain of walking through Andy's death again will be worth the agony.

When I began this project, my goal was simply to finish the story and hopefully find some answers to the question, 'Why'. I did not have any plans on publishing a book. As a novice at writing, I had no idea how to even begin to write my story. By coincidence, I read about a publishing class being offered at Paradise Valley College. In this class I met the instructor, Ralph Tanner. With his encouragement and advice I was able to develop a format for my story, and could sit down and begin. Mr. Tanner continued to take me under his wing, and direct my work. Upon completing the story he was kind enough to offer to read the rough draft. After reading the draft, he felt the story was one that concerned parents and professionals should hear about, and that there was a message that should be shared. Through Mr. Tanner's connections, we produced/aired two thirty-minute television interviews last Fall. The television station, KUSK in Prescott, was so moved by my story and tragedy of suicide, they decided to produce a one hour documentary on adolescent suicide. This one hour special was completed and aired May 13, 2000.

In the television special, U. S. Surgeon General David Satcher speaks to the epidemic of adolescent suicide in the United States; and in July 1999, he issued a *Call to Action* to prevent adolescent suicide. Judge Portley, a juvenile court judge in Phoenix, gave generously of his time. He is very active in his tireless effort to help juveniles improve the quality of their lives. Youth suicide is beginning to come out of the closet, as more and more people share their stories and heartbreak. I have been privileged to meet some of these people, and find that we all have a common goal. We do not want anyone else to suffer the lifelong pain we have had to experience.

As a response to these survivors of suicide, and with their encouragement, I have developed a nonprofit organization: Youth Suicide Prevention Education Program. The concept of the organization is designed to concentrate on prevention. And educate mental health professionals, educators in particular, parents and the public about the warning signs, and perhaps help prevent suicide.

Joyce Gatson
Phoenix, Arizona
May 2000

Contents

Andy's Death

I heard what sounded like an exploding firecracker. The time was 2:30 a.m., and I had been in and out of bed all night, worrying about Andy. I lay there in bed for a moment, and thought, no, the sound was a gunshot. My next thought was, Andy has shot himself. Getting out of bed, I walked through the house toward the Arizona room. The Arizona room is located in the back of the house and was designated as Andy's 'recreation' room, where he and his friends could 'hang out' and have privacy.

As I walked through the kitchen, I looked from the kitchen window into the Arizona room. The light was on and Andy appeared to be sitting in his usual place on the sofa, next to the telephone. I could not see what he was doing so I continued to walk through the kitchen doorway, through the utility area, to the doorway of the Arizona room. At first glance he appeared to have fallen asleep sitting upright. His eyes were closed, a peaceful look on his face. I then saw the gun resting in his lap, and saw pieces of brain matter on his chest. I could not make myself go any closer, thinking, "Andy is dead, his pain has ended." In the same moment Andy's presence seemed to be hovering just above the scene, looking at me and at his body. Andy's spirit appeared confused, unable to understand what had taken place.

My first response was to walk back to the bedroom, knowing in my heart that he was dead. I screamed and continued screaming until my husband, Mike, came stumbling to the doorway looking startled and agitated. I cried out to Mike telling him Andy had shot himself. Mike rushed to the Arizona room where Andy sat so peacefully on the sofa. My memory is vague whether Mike told me to dial 911 or if my response was automatic. The 911 operator answered within a few rings and I told her my son had shot himself. My feelings toward her were becoming hostile as she kept telling me to be calm, as though talking to a child. My voice was shaking, and I could hardly speak; shock had already placed me on autopilot. The operator kept me on the telephone while she dispatched an ambulance to our home. She asked if Andy was breathing. I did not know. Mike checked, and told me Andy was breathing a rattling kind of breath. The operator then told me to get a cloth and press the cloth against the wound. The message was relayed to Mike and he brought a clean cloth and pressed the material to his son's wound until the paramedics arrived. Mike stayed in the Arizona room holding the cloth to Andy's head while I remained on the telephone with the 911 operator.

An EMT ambulance arrived within five minutes, the firehouse is two blocks away. The operator allowed me to hang up the telephone when she was told the paramedics were in the house. No siren was used when the paramedics arrived and they came quietly into the house. I could not bring myself to go back into the Arizona room. Mike stayed with Andy until the paramedics relieved him. The EMTs worked quickly and carefully with Andy. One paramedic asked Mike to remove the gun from Andy's lap. They did not want to touch the gun.

Andy's body was placed on the floor as the EMTs performed their emergency procedures. They were methodical in attending Andy, apparently in no rush to take him to the hospital, confirming in my mind what my heart already knew. Andy was dead.

The police came about the same time the paramedics arrived. My guess is the 911 operators automatically notify the police when a shooting occurs. The officers asked Mike and me to sit while they talked with us. We sat at the kitchen table as the police asked the necessary questions. At the time, I was in shock, and felt as though I was outside my body, watching my responses and those of the people around me. The police asked us questions about Andy's state of mind, and what he had been doing that night. An officer brought us a carbon copy of a citation that had been lying on the coffee table in the Arizona room. He asked if we had seen the citation, and we said 'no'. The ticket was for speeding and drunk driving. The police had stopped Andy for speeding earlier in the evening, four blocks from home, and arrested him for drunk driving. The officer drove him to the Squaw Peak police station for questioning. At the station, he told the policeman he was upset about having broken up with his girl friend.

Later, this same officer told us Andy was a very pleasant young man, polite and cooperative. We already knew that. After the police checked Andy's record for outstanding warrants, he was sent home in a taxi. The taxi driver apparently brought him home and waited while he picked up an extra set of keys to his car. The driver then drove Andy to his car, and in the car was a gun. The arresting officer later told us he had seen the gun on the dashboard of the car. However, since carrying a weapon in the open is legal in Arizona, the officer did nothing about the gun. To my knowledge, at the time,

3

Andy did not own a gun. He was well aware of my opposition to firearms.

The investigating officers completed the police report about the same time the paramedics finished placing Andy into the ambulance. My thought was that the paramedics had been very slow in getting Andy into the ambulance, but as mentioned earlier, they probably knew that there was no hurry. Andy was dead, even if he was still breathing. The paramedics asked us if we could drive to St. Joseph's Hospital ER and if so, they would meet us there. We replied that we could drive ourselves to the hospital.

Mike and I drove to the hospital in Mike's truck, not speaking. Emotionally, I was beginning to withdraw from the reality of Andy's death. St. Joseph's ER was in the middle of renovation, and we were placed in a small bare room furnished with two stiff backed chairs. During that time, Mike and I talked about family and friends we should notify. About thirty minutes passed before the doctors came in to talk with us. They came solemnly into the room and confirmed what Mike and I already knew: Andy was brain dead. In Arizona the medical authorities declare a person dead if there is no brain wave activity. Andy fit the legal criteria for brain death although he was still breathing, and his organs functioning. The doctors explained to us that the heart and organs would continue to function for several hours without life support, or signals from the brain.

The doctors asked us if we would consider organ donation. Mike and I took one look at each other and said 'yes'. They suggested we take a few minutes to consider our decision, but we assured them we did not need the time. In the past Mike and I had talked about organ donation and agreed that if possible we would like to donate our organs when we died. We

4

had never talked about donating our son's organs. In the natural order of things, Andy should be the one burying us, not us him. In my mind, donating Andy's organs would provide some good in an otherwise senseless and tragic waste of life. Thinking back, perhaps our decision to donate his organs was a way for us to hold on to him, of keeping him alive, even if that life was in other people's bodies.

The doctors asked us to wait while they prepared and dressed Andy and put him on life support systems. The doctors explained that Andy would be on life support until the Donor Network could find recipients for his organs. The matching of recipients to the donor's organs is a comprehensive process. The Donor Network is responsible for finding suitable recipients through a nationwide computerized waiting list. The doctors also explained the process could take eight hours or more to match Andy's organs with compatible recipients. They asked if we wanted to wait with him during this time. We could see no advantage in waiting with his body. In my mind his spirit had left his body when I first saw him in the Arizona room. All that was left behind now was the physical shell he had worn. Andy was no longer residing in his body. I wish now we had stayed with Andy for a few hours, but at the time, I could not bear looking at my baby and knowing he was dead.

The staff at St. Joseph's ER had asked us when we arrived in the emergency room if we wanted a pastor or priest present. We asked them to contact a priest. A priest came into the room to see us shortly after the doctors left, and he took us to the cafeteria for coffee. We did not know him personally. He was a chaplain assigned to be on call for emergencies at the hospital. The three of us spoke for a short time about life and death, until the nurse came to take Mike and me to see Andy.

The nurse was very kind, and she tried to prepare us for what we would see. She told us to say anything we wanted to Andy; she explained that scientific studies have shown that the ability to hear is one of the last functions a body loses. However, she said that medical science does not know how much a patient hears while they are unconscious. The nurse had tears in her eyes and was holding me tightly with both arms around me as we walked along the corridor. Tears were running down my face and there was a huge lump in my throat. My voice was little more than a whisper. Apparently my throat had been strained when I screamed after seeing Andy in the Arizona room. My legs were shaky but I was able to walk. Mike had tears in his eyes, and was crying silently. The nurse continued to console and advise us while we walked through the double doors of the emergency room. She told us Andy was hooked up to life support machines, and that his eyelids would be swollen due to the rupture of the blood vessels in his eyes from the gunshot. She assured us Andy could feel no pain from his head wound.

We went through the doors into a room filled with medical equipment, and there lay my baby. Andy had a breathing apparatus in his mouth, tubes everywhere. His eyelids were bulging, and his mop of unruly curly hair lay on the pillow around his head. A security guard was standing a few feet from Andy. The presence of the guard was intimidating. A stranger had no right to see and hear my grief. In spite of the guard's presence, I held Andy in my arms, and told him how much he was loved and that he was forgiven for this tragic act. As Mike took his turn crying and telling his son how much he loved him, I stood to one side and wept at the sight. We both cried openly as the guard stood by sadly. The nurse never left my side. After a brief period with Andy, we were ready to leave him.

The nurse escorted us back to the emergency room entrance we had entered a few hours earlier.

As we drove home, we talked about what arrangements we should make in the next few days. We agreed we wanted to cremate Andy's remains. We decided to have a memorial service for him at St. Francis Xavier Church where we attended and where Andy had been an altar boy.

After arriving home I called Tim, Andy's friend who he had been out with that night. The time was 5:30 a.m., and Tim's father answered the telephone. I told him what happened to Andy, and he woke Tim right away. After talking to Tim, he insisted upon coming immediately to our home to be with us.

The police returned to our house later the same morning with the final report of their investigation. The officers were very kind and gentle as they went over the report with us. Their finding was that Andy had died from a self-inflicted wound to the head. My memory is not clear whether we signed any paper work as a legal formality. As we were finishing with the police, Tim arrived. We introduced him to the officers, and they took their leave. Mike and I explained to Tim what had happened in more detail about Andy's death. We told Tim we had agreed to donate Andy's organs, and he was being kept on life support until the harvest of his organs was completed. Tim asked us what he could do to help. We asked him to take Andy's address book and call their friends to tell them of his death. Tim agreed to do this task for us, and with Andy's address book in hand he returned to his home.

Mike and I waited for about an hour after Tim left before calling any members of Mike's family. I have no idea what we did during that hour. My guess is that we sat together and prayed for our son. Prayer had always been a big part of our lives, especially Mike's, and we really needed to pray for the strength to get through this nightmare. About 6:30 a.m. Mike called his sister, Peggy, and told her of Andy's death. Peggy was stunned, but told Mike she would take care of calling the other family members, and someone would be over to stay with us as soon as possible.

Within thirty minutes after calling Peggy, Mike's oldest niece, Rita, was at our door. She stayed with us until Peggy and Janie, Mike's youngest sister, came to be with us. Peggy and Janie were a godsend. The sisters fielded telephone calls, cleaned the house, and stayed with us during the days until the memorial services for Andy the following Saturday.

Sometime after we had returned home from the hospital, I called my sister in California and my stepfather in Washington to tell them of Andy's death. Both had poor health and would be unable to come to Arizona to be with us. Also, I telephoned a few of my friends, locally and out of state, to advise them of Andy's death. My reactions were those of a robot, displaying no emotion, and functioning as if mechanical. My throat continued to ache from the stress, and my behavior during the days leading up to Andy's memorial service was subdued and erratic. During the coming days Mike seemed to cry more; tears were often streaming down his cheeks. My concerned sisters-in-law kept watching me as though they expected me to become hysterical. In my mind the situation seemed grimly humorous the way everyone kept discreetly watching me to see if I were going to fall apart. Unfortunately, showing my emotions to others is not something that comes easily. As a child, I learned to share my joy and happiness, but sharing my pain was an imposition on others.

After calling the family Mike and I called our parish church, St. Francis Xavier, and asked for Father Wright to contact us. He soon returned our telephone call and we told him of

Andy's death. He said he would come to see us about eleven o'clock that morning. We knew Fr. Wright personally, and I liked the compassion and dry humor he showed toward his parishioners. Fr. Wright knew Andy and me from the years I had taught at St. Francis Elementary School. Mike and I were aware Fr. Wright had suffered a devastating loss of loved ones before he became a priest and would understand what we were going through.

Fr. Wright came to the house to comfort us and to help make arrangements for religious services for Andy. Andy's body was to be cremated, so there would be no casket or burial plot. We definitely wanted a memorial service for him at St. Francis Church. Fr. Wright suggested we move as quickly as possible in having the service, so as not to prolong our pain. Many Catholics hold a rosary service the day before a funeral. My impulse was to have a rosary service for Andy, but Fr. Wright counseled against putting ourselves through two emotionally draining religious services. Mike and I agreed with his recommendations. The nightmare of Andy's death began the Thursday morning of his suicide; the memorial service was held Saturday evening, August 6, 1994, two days after his death. Saturday night is 'party night', so having Andy's service on a Saturday night seemed fitting. Andy loved a party, and we wanted his short life to be a celebration.

On Friday, Peggy and Janie accompanied Mike and me to the funeral home to make final arrangements. The funeral director was very kind and counseled us to be conservative with the funeral service and arrangements. Subsequently, arrangements for the memorial service were kept simple. Mike and I could not decide what type of urn we wanted for Andy's ashes. The funeral director suggested we wait to decide about the urn and we accepted his advice.

The caring response from friends and family on learning about Andy's death was truly amazing. We had not realized our small family had so many friends. Everyone was shocked about the death and supportive in our grief. Mike's dear friends who live in San Diego and Belmont, California, arranged to fly in for Andy's memorial service. The cards and notes of condolence came flooding into our home. Andy has enough perpetual prayers being said for him for the next millennium. Many people we know are Catholic and they knew that our family was Catholic. Often Catholic religious orders provide perpetual prayers when people request them. Although the custom of requesting perpetual prayers was not familiar to me, I am now very thankful for the tradition. After a religious order receives a request for prayers, a beautiful card is sent advising the bereaved their loved one will forever be included in daily prayers. The religious order includes the name of the donor who has asked for the prayers for the deceased loved one, so the family is made aware of the contributors. These prayers give me great comfort in knowing that not only Mike and I pray for Andy daily, but many others are also praying for him.

The number of friends at the church Saturday evening for the memorial service amazed me. The church altar was covered with floral arrangements. Previously, I had gone to a florist to arrange for a picture of Andy to be centered on an easel with flowers around his photograph. The easel was placed on the altar for people to view and remember their relationship with Andy. Approximately five hundred people attended and signed the memorial book we had in the foyer. Probably half the people attending were Andy's friends, and the rest were friends of Mike and me. Although not planned, I stood in the foyer and greeted people coming into the church for the service. Mike stood on the other side of the foyer. My memory of the service is of all the names and faces of people who came to share their condolences. Andy's grammar school teachers from St. Francis were there, including the principal. Also, the pastor of St. Francis Church, friends from our places of employment, and Mike's family and our close friends were present. We did not know half the young people who were sitting in the pews, but they all knew Andy. These young people were weeping and those who knew me hugged me and acknowledged Mike.

Our niece, Rita, had volunteered to handle the funeral service arrangements. Mike and I told her what music we wanted, and that we wanted the youth ministry musicians to sing. The rest of the service was in her hands. Rita presented a brief eulogy and she arranged for Tim Sundberg, Andy's friend, and Bill Marcotte his church sponsor, to say a few words.

Bill had been Andy's sponsor for his confirmation as a Catholic at age seventeen. Bill is very involved in the Catholic charismatic community here in Arizona, and believes suicide is a mortal sin. Bill prayed about whether he should speak at the service. As a result of prayer, Bill felt God gave him a verse which says 'forgive them, for they know not what they do'. He shared this verse during his words about Andy.

Rita shared her affection for Andy and recalled the summer he attended a Young Life camp where she was a counselor. She said that many of the young people at the camp would come to her and say that Andy was pleasant and funny. Until that summer trip Rita never really knew her cousin.

Tim spoke for many of Andy's friends. He had discussed his part of the eulogy with several of them prior to the service and they had agreed on what Tim was to say: "There are no words that can accurately describe how much Andy meant to us. He had a big heart and he was always there for his friends. Andy never backed off from helping someone in need and by doing that he brought out the best in all of us. He lived life on his own terms and showed us all what a true friend should be. His warm smile and boisterous laugh will be remembered. Andy's spirit will always be with us, and his presence will be sorely missed. We love you Andy."

I surprised everyone, and startled Fr. Wright, by stumbling to the podium. After listening to the weeping youth in the audience, my need was to comfort them. They should know that Andy loved them, and that I loved them and wanted them to feel free to come to our home to see us if they needed to talk. After my spontaneous speech, even the men were crying. Fr. Wright helped me to my seat and the services were concluded.

We had a simple reception at our home. My thought was to have a party for Andy, but Mike wanted the reception simple. Many of the young people came, expressed their grief and quietly took their leave. No one stayed long. Soon, Mike and I were left to grieve together.

Andrew Banning Gatson
July 19, 1973 - August 4, 1994
Born: San Francisco, California
Died: Phoenix, Arizona
Age: 21
"His warm smile and boisterous
laugh will be remembered."

[2]

The Beginning

In an effort to understand Andy's death I need to begin by examining my own life; as a youngster and as an adult. My sincere belief is that by examining my own past and environment I can create a history of how my life influenced Andy's life.

This personal history is not an attempt to rationalize Andy's death, but rather an attempt to find a reason and/or understand the choices Andy made.

The story of Andy is an attempt to examine how and why this beautiful young man is dead by his own hand. As parents, could his father and I have prevented his death? Was the suicide inevitable? Was his death anyone's fault? I will always blame myself, because his frailty was similar to mine, and I was unable to give him the skills he needed to survive in this complex world. The only difference in our personalities is my mother made me tough, a fighter. Maybe that is why I am still here, and Andy is gone. There is no knowledge of why he died. Perhaps, we will learn that truth when we meet again in a better place. Only then will I really be able to understand and accept his death. Until then, I must learn to live with my grief, and find some reason to wait until that moment when we can be together again.

Where to begin my story? Children have always been very special to me. My sisters are older, and when I was only ten years old they began their families. I was drawn to their children, loving them very much. My nieces and nephews suffered because of their parents' personal problems and this troubled me. Seeing children suffer and how hard the job of parenting seemed to be, I began to question parenthood when very young.

I was the fourth child born into a very poor and unhappy family. My parents were migrants from Arkansas, who moved to California in the late thirties to work in the farm fields. My parents personified the image written in the *Grapes of Wrath* by John Steinbeck. The people migrating to California during the depression were called 'Okies' and 'Arkies' and treated just as badly as today's migrant workers. My parents were married as teenagers, and both lived and worked on farms in Arkansas until the drought in the Midwest and the depression of the thirties forced them to pack up their three children and seek work in the lush fields of California. My mother's parents and her siblings came with her and my father in an old Model 'A' truck, with a mattress on the flatbed. The entire family ended up in the verdant fields of the San Joaquin Valley. There they worked the crops, picking cotton, walnuts, grapes and the other fruit and vegetables that grew in the fields.

In 1940, about a year after my parents moved to California I was born in Hanford. My memory as a little girl was of sitting on the end of my mother's cotton sack as she worked her way through the fields. The children were allowed to go with their parents to the fields, and we ran happily through the rows of crops, playing and not realizing how hard our parents were working. Another memory is of a beautiful sun-drenched day spent playing in the cotton fields with the other children and jumping off the side of a cotton bin into the freshly picked cotton. The feeling was like jumping into the clouds. Sometimes we would land on a prickly cotton boll. Most of the time the cotton was soft and we jumped on the pile as children would on a mattress.

When the cannery in Armona opened my mother got a job working on the assembly line, and I attended a preschool provided for the workers' children by the cannery. My memories of the school are pleasant, although my attendance was for a short time. My family moved around the countryside, following the seasons. Sometimes we lived in a tent or a one-room house provided for the pickers. My mother worked in the fields beside my father, and could pick as much of the crop as he, earning as much as he did, a dollar a day. The family problems began on the weekends when my father would take their hard-earned money and squander the money on alcohol and gambling. My mother would rant and rave, and even throw things, but she never left him.

My three older siblings were born in Arkansas and were much older. There were two girls and a boy, each about two years apart in age. Because of the age difference between me and my siblings, I was often lonely; until my mother gave birth to a girl when I was two and a half years old. Now I had a sister, Georgianna, to love and take care of and we were a family. My oldest sister, Dolores, was sixteen and baby-sat Georgianna and me. Dolores had a terrible temper and would hit us when we were not doing what she wanted. Because of her behavior, I felt a need to protect Georgianna. In today's society Dolores would be accused of child abuse, but in those days slapping and spanking children was considered a family right.

In 1946, when Georgianna was two and a half years old she was scratched by a stray cat; the scratch became infected and she soon went into a coma. She was taken to the hospital where she died two days later having never regained consciousness. As a five-year-old I was devastated by Georgianna's death. My mother became hysterical at the funeral and had to be carried from the service. I was lost and forgotten in all the sorrow. No one even noticed me or consoled me. My memory to this day is of my little sister dressed in blue silk lying on white satin in her coffin. My thinking at that time was that the wrong child had died. I should have been the one to die, since everyone loved her so much. My mourning for Georgianna's death lasted for many years. Never again could I attend a funeral without suffering a flashback of seeing my baby sister lying in her casket, and feeling again all the pain of so long ago.

Six months after my sister died, my mother in her pain and suffering from the death of her baby, divorced my father. My father never believed my mother would ever divorce him, although she had threatened to leave him for seventeen years because of his drinking and gambling. He was shocked by the divorce and moved back to Arkansas where his parents and relatives lived. He remarried within a year to a widow with two teenage daughters. The children in my immediate family stayed with my mother in California. My oldest sister was living on her own, and my brother and sister were in high school and lived with Mom and me. My mother raised me to think bringing children into this world was an awesome responsibility. With all the pain and suffering that goes on in this world, is one being fair to bring a child into this vale of tears?

My older siblings were teenagers and very rebellious. My brother, Doyle, eventually moved to Arkansas to be with our father. My two sisters stayed in California with Mom and me. The girls could not get along with one another or with our mother; so my mother gave up on them and set her sights on raising me 'right'. To this end, mother and I moved to Fresno, a larger city than Hanford. Another factor was while living in Hanford, mother had met a very nice man, from Fresno, and she wanted to be near him. Also, she wanted to take me away from the small-town environment. The move turned out to be a positive one for me.

Three years later my mother married that same nice man, and he provided a solid foundation for a child who had never known people could live in peace and love. Their marriage was not without problems, but they stayed together for almost thirty years before my mother died. Giving much of the credit to my stepfather and his family, I am the only member of my family to have graduated from college. My success at attending college can be attributed to the fact my stepfather was a quiet, intelligent man who loved to read. Perhaps he encouraged me because his only son had just finished college when he and my mother were married. My stepfather's family was always kind to me, and he treated me as his daughter. He is alive today, and our close father-daughter relationship continues to be a source of pleasure.

As a youngster my summers were spent, whenever possible, with my biological father and stepmother in Arkansas. I loved my irresponsible father very much. Dad was warm, loving, and boyish. He always worked hard, but could never manage his money. He was generous and could easily be taken advantage of by any hard luck story. Dad loved cars and was always buying a different model each year. He made me feel loved and special during my summers with him. My stepmother had two daughters of her own and they were always pleasant to me. I was a child who responded well to being treated kindly.

My need was for everyone to like me and I made an effort to please people. My father came from a family of twelve children and his relatives lived in Arkansas, providing us with a large family for gatherings and fun. They were an active loving family, and summers were spent with Sunday get togethers. Most of the relatives lived in the country on farms and on Sundays would gather at one of the houses to eat fried chicken, homemade pie and ice cream. My Aunt Lola could make the best homemade pies ever tasted, and the ice cream was made with real cream. No ice cream from a store could come close to the taste of old-fashioned homemade ice cream. My Aunt Lola was my favorite aunt. She and Uncle Floyd, her husband, moved back and forth between Arkansas and California as my uncle's work in farming required. Whenever they came back to California, Aunt Lola would take care of me after school while my mother was at work. Her homes in Arkansas and California were my favorite places to visit.

After graduating from high school in Fresno, at the age of seventeen, I started work for the telephone company as a switchboard operator. A year later, I transferred within the system to Arkansas to be with my father.

In 1960, after a year in Arkansas, I missed my home and friends in California and resigned from the telephone company to return to Fresno. After returning to Fresno, determined to advance my career, I began work with an insurance company. At the insurance company my progress from typist to office manager came within two years. The achievement was very rewarding to me and I continued working in the insurance field for fifteen years.

In 1961 many of my friends were getting married. They

married at eighteen or nineteen years of age and I was considered an oddball for remaining single. At the age of twenty-one, I finally succumbed to everyone's pressure to get married and married my cousin's boy friend, which did not make me very popular with my cousin. Bob and I had known each other for over a year, but only dated two months before we were married.

We moved to San Jose, because he worked for an electronics company located there. Soon after arriving, Bob became tired of his job and decided he wanted to go to school. I offered to continue working and support his college education. However, after three years of college, he could not decide what he wanted to do professionally. Eventually, his indecision and his irresponsible behavior became factors in our divorce. In many ways Bob was similar to my biological father; easygoing, kind and immature. He was always very good to me and we had an amicable divorce. Shortly after our divorce my employer closed the office in Fresno and relocated to San Francisco. Being unemployed and divorced, my decision was to leave Fresno and move to San Francisco to stay in the insurance industry. I remained there for two years before returning to Fresno to finish college. I had been taking night classes over the previous ten years, but at that rate figured to be an old lady before receiving my degree. The insurance business had become tiresome and my plan was to become a teacher. My love for children persuaded me to focus on teaching elementary school.

After the move to San Francisco I lived in a residence club in Pacific Heights. Some of the old Victorian mansions had been converted into residence clubs by the owners, providing room and board for the renters. My residence club was called the Astonia and was a beautiful old mansion located in the middle of Pacific Heights; now a very exclusive neighborhood in San Francisco. The boarding house was perfect for me. I could pay my rent and have two meals a day and a comfortable place to sleep. There were young people from all over the world staying in the Astonia and living there was a wonderful way to meet people.

The Astonia is where my present husband Mike and I met. He had moved to San Francisco from Phoenix a few months earlier than me. For me, breakfast was a nuisance, although I was usually home from work for the evening meal. The dinners were served family style, and the diners sat at any table where there was a vacant place. One night Mike and I happened to share the same table. Later in the week there was a party in one of the rooms and I went to see what was happening. Mike was there. The people at the party soon decided to go to another location. Mike and I did not want to go with them so we went out together, and that is how our relationship began. We dated exclusively for a year and a half. Neither of us was ready to make a commitment, and my decision was to attend college. Mike encouraged me to pursue college even though this meant my moving back to Fresno where expenses would be less. We tried to continue a long-distance relationship, but to no avail. Within a few months of my returning to Fresno we were no longer seeing each other on a regular basis.

For the next two years I happily pursued my education and worked full-time to support myself. I lived on a limited budget, working thirty-five hours a week, carrying a minimum of eighteen credit hours, and was never happier in my life. My self-esteem had been battered after failing in my first marriage, and going to college made me feel better about myself. I was almost thirty years old and felt there was a possibility of never marrying again. In Fresno I made good friends, and dated occasionally, but nothing serious in the relationship department.

At thirty years of age, the biological urge to have a child of my own became important to me. However, my belief was that a child needed a mother and father, the old 'traditional family' myth. Mike had continued to stay in touch while I was in college, and he came back into my life during my junior year. Mike, now settled in his career, was ready to make the commitment to marriage.

To explain Mike's history briefly, he was born in St. Louis and moved with his family to Arizona for his mother's health when Mike was eight years old. Mike's mother had rheumatoid arthritis of the spine and was in a wheelchair by the time she was twenty-eight years of age. In addition to Mike there were three sisters, one older and two younger. When Mike was sixteen, his mother gave birth to another son. This event surprised the family, because she had been in a wheelchair for almost ten years. Mike's maternal grandmother, Nana, moved with them from St. Louis to Phoenix to help care for Mike's mother and the children. Mike's father was a postman. The family was old-fashioned Irish Catholic. Mike's maternal grandfather migrated from Ireland, and Nana had come from Germany. Mike attended parochial school through high school, and graduated from Arizona State University with a degree in business administration. After working in Phoenix at temporary jobs Mike attended the American Institute for International Business. He could not afford to complete the graduate program and decided to move to San Francisco to pursue a career in the import-export business.

Mike's close relationship with his family and the fact that his parents had never divorced, was impressive to me. The family seemed very loving and caring. They were the type of family I always wanted to share. Mike had a confidence and self-assurance about him which made me feel safe and secure. My thinking was that coming from such a wonderful family, he would be a good husband and father.

After we started dating again, Mike was eager to be married. The commute every weekend from San Francisco to Fresno to see me was tiring for him. Within six months of our renewed dating we decided to be married before I completed college. This required my return to San Francisco. We were married quietly, telling only our family members and my close friends. Mike did not want to tell his friends in advance of the ceremony, wanting to surprise them. Also, we preferred a small wedding. One weekend in April 1971 we drove to Virginia City, Nevada, and were married. Four months later we had another simple ceremony in the Catholic church in Fresno where I had completed my religious conversion to Catholicism.

I was never raised in any particular religion, and attended many different churches when young. My father was a Baptist and my best friends as a child were Catholic. During my teenage years most of my friends were Protestant. My mother never believed in organized religion, and my stepfather was an agnostic. My belief was that a child needed a spiritual foundation, and thought the best way for this foundation to be laid was if both parents were of the same religion. Although drawn to the Catholic religion, I found some of the dogma of the earlier church impossible for me to accept. After the Vatican II Council in 1965, much of the dogma in the Catholic faith was changed and became acceptable to me.

My one stipulation to the marriage with Mike had been to complete my bachelor's degree before returning to work. After completing my degree at Cal State Hayward I began working for an insurance broker as an account assistant. Another year of college was required to obtain my teaching certificate, but Mike and I agreed to put my education on hold until we were financially secure. We decided not to wait too long for children, because of our ages; mine in particular. My preference was for several children, preferably two boys. Mike was enjoying our lifestyle, and he was unsure if he even wanted children. Within a few months, with due consideration, he agreed that having children would complete our family.

Two months after becoming pregnant I began having physical problems and a medical examination showed an ectopic pregnancy and required a dilatation and curettage. Six months later I was again pregnant. We were ecstatic. My health was wonderful during my pregnancy, never suffering a day of morning sickness. As a precaution I gave up drinking alcohol. This was before research in child development really proved that alcohol was extremely harmful for a fetus. My concern was that my child's development should not be affected by alcohol. I worked in downtown San Francisco until the day a sudden complication in my pregnancy caused me to be rushed to Mt. Zion Hospital in a taxi. The driver who took me from my office to the hospital was very nervous about my imminent condition.

Our child was born six weeks early, and on the day of delivery nothing about the birth seemed to go right. There was no labor or dilation and Andy remained in a breech position. The doctors waited three hours to see if labor would begin, but when there were no contractions they decided to perform a caesarean. The most important issue to me at the time was for Andy to be safe. I was willing to do anything necessary to make sure he was a healthy baby. Andy was born on Wednesday at 3:00 p.m. on July 19, 1973. A spinal block allowed me to be conscious during Andy's birth. This procedure enabled me to see his beautiful face before the nurses carried him to intensive care. The doctors then gave me anesthesia before closing my incision. On regaining consciousness, a nurse advised me not to move for twelve hours because of the spinal block. The inability to see Andy immediately was very distressing for me.

The doctor told me that Andy was doing fine, weighing five pounds, six ounces, but needed to remain in intensive care as a precautionary measure against infection. As soon as possible, twelve hours later, I went to see him. He was so beautiful. As a result of the caesarean birth, his head was perfectly formed, his skin tone light pink. He had a full head of hair, medium brown in color. His eyes were like saucers, blue in color, with long curly lashes. Mike was allowed to see and hold him, too. We were both proud and excited. Mike was an emotional mess; he was so accustomed to me taking care of everything at home that he could not even find the coffee pot. In anticipation of Andy's birth we borrowed a handmade cradle from the VanLuewens, a wonderful Dutch family we knew. The cradle was a welcome place for our baby. The women in my office had given me a surprise baby shower just two days before Andy was born. Pregnant women were not seen often in downtown San Francisco, and Andy's birth was a big deal to an office staff of two hundred or more people. My office had a betting pool going on the date and hour of his birth.

My stay in the hospital was seven days, but Andy had to stay another few days because he became jaundiced. In the hospital ICU, I attempted to breast-feed Andy, looking forward to the bonding experience. He was not a willing recipient. In intensive care he had been given a bottle which was much easier for him to nurse. He had to be fed every two hours because he was premature. My breast milk was adequate and the doctors encouraged me to nurse Andy explaining that a mother's milk had more natural nutrients that an infant need-ed for growth. After three months of trying to persuade him to nurse, I gave up and bottle fed him. Andy had caught up in weight and size and the doctors said he would be all right on a formula and bottle. Of course, there was disappointment about missing the experience of nursing my child. Andy was always held during feeding, so that he would get the same warmth and stimulation whether feeding from a breast or a bottle. At home we had a rocking chair where I usually sat to nurse him.

In my mind not being able to breast-feed Andy was a failing. I had wanted natural childbirth, with Mike at my side. Instead the birth was a caesarean, and Mike was left out of the entire process. The birth was expected to be a wonderful experi-ence for all of us, bonding with our child, nursing Andy from my own breast. At the time the caesarean was performed my concerns were not about experiencing natural childbirth but Andy's welfare. Yet, my determination was to be the perfect wife and mother, in spite of these setbacks.

Mike picked out Andy's name. My suggestion was to use my maiden name, Howard, for Andy's middle name, but Mike did not think the name would compliment the name Andrew. We found the name "Banning," meaning "Gaelic warrior," in a baby book. We decided "Banning" was a good middle name. The thought that *our child* would be any gender other than a boy never crossed our minds, so we never looked at names for girls. Prior to Andy's birth, Mike's friends shared their versions of gender selection, but as a wife and expectant mother I knew that male ego would not be a factor.

Andy was a sweet baby, gaining weight and developing well within the normal ranges of any infant. By the time he was five months old, he had caught up in size and weight to a full-term baby. And he finally started sleeping through the night. He was a good sleeper, but needed to eat every two hours for the first few months, and then every four hours, until five months old. At this time Mike and I decided to fly to Phoenix for Christmas and show off our new son. My sister-in-law Judy, who lived in Phoenix had given birth to a son, Michael, about six weeks after Andy was born.

The trip was unfortunate because Andy contracted a virus by being exposed to so many people in Phoenix; by the time we flew home to San Francisco we had a very sick baby. As a precaution, the pediatricians were called and they gave me a prescription for Andy, but the medicine did not help. Andy had diarrhea so severe that after three days he became dehydrated, and was admitted to the hospital for intravenous feeding. In the hospital his screaming could be heard from down the hall where the nurses had sent me while they inserted the intravenous needle in his little forehead. Fortunately, Mt. Zion was a teaching hospital, and the staff was very progressive in children's healthcare. They allowed me to stay with Andy at the hospital twenty-four hours a day. The nurses understood that an infant is better off with the mother near, and encouraged mothers to stay with their sick children as much as possible. Andy was in the hospital three to five days. Finally, he stabilized, taking in fluids and retaining them in his tiny body. Once Andy was home, our life returned to normal.

Andy started rocking when he was five or six months old. He would get on his knees with his head down on the mattress and rock forward and backward. This action would scoot his little body up to the head of the crib, where he would continue to rock, hitting his head against the crib headboard. There were bumper pads around the inside of his crib, but we still worried about Andy hurting himself. The pediatrician assured me rocking was simply a soothing type of behavior, like sucking the thumb or sucking on a blanket. Sometimes his rocking would move the crib completely across the room, until a wall stopped the crib. Andy continued this behavior until he was much older, when he substituted the rocking with thumping one leg on the bed until he fell asleep. He never cried or fussed at these times, seeming content to rock himself to sleep.

Andy was about eight months old when he developed bronchitis and had to be hospitalized again. He was placed in an oxygen tent, and within a few days was fully recovered. Once again I stayed with him, but one night went home to rest, because he seemed to be doing so well. On my arrival at the hospital the next morning he was screaming, and no nurse was anywhere to be found. I was furious with the nurses, and felt very guilty for leaving him. After giving them a piece of my mind, I calmed down, and took him home.

When Andy started crawling he became frustrated very easily and would simply give up when he met an obstacle that interfered with his progress. No amount of encouragement helped him; he would simply cry until someone removed the difficulty. As early as six months of age if he was upset, or ate too much, he would vomit immediately. After speaking with his pediatricians about the vomiting and bronchial problems, they explained to me that the respiratory and digestive systems are the last to fully develop in a premature child. Subsequently, they said Andy's vulnerability to illness would manifest in his digestive and respiratory systems. This prophetic statement turned out to be very true. Throughout Andy's life, his illnesses were related to respiratory or digestive problems.

In reference to Andy's pediatricians: they were wonderful,

and very progressive for that era. In this medical practice four doctors were in partnership and someone was available day or night if a parent had a sick child or a question. The doctors offered a one year health contract that parents could buy for a basic fee. This contract covered the usual infant visits and a patient could have as many additional visits to the doctor as needed at no increased cost. As a first time parent, this contract gave me much comfort and ended up saving us a great deal of money that first year.

Andy started walking at twelve months of age and was a delightful baby. He took a nap every morning and afternoon, and in the evening would go to bed by himself when he was tired. He was easy to discipline, with a simple 'no' being enough to halt unruly behavior. He continued to be very sensitive in his environment and easily upset by stress; any unpleasant incident caused him to promptly throw up. Mike and I became accustomed to Andy vomiting and neither of us would make an issue about cleaning up a mess.

While we were living in San Francisco there was a young Chinese couple with two daughters living next door to us. When Andy was about two years of age, there was an incident with the two little girls. The girls were around the age of Andy, one slightly older, the other younger. The children were playing together outside and the girls hit Andy. Instead of hitting the girls back, he came running to us not knowing how to react to violence. We tried to explain that some children hit and he was permitted to defend himself. His response to the girls seemed to us as a little unusual for a two-year-old child; most children that age would have simply struck back.

Andy even cried the first time he saw cartoons depicting violence, he was only a toddler at the time. I never cared much for television, and allowed Andy to watch Sesame Street occasionally. We preferred reading to him, or having him play inside or outside the house. To illustrate his response to rejection, another incident occurred when he was two or three years old. The three of us went to see my family in Fresno and were visiting my sister. She enjoys teasing in fun and when Andy opened a cupboard door to see inside, the door came off, and she jokingly said, "look what you did." At this comment Andy burst into tears and began throwing up. My sister was shocked and felt terrible about having upset him. His responses to situations similar to this made Mike and me realize we had a very sensitive child on our hands. We did not realize how much distress this condition would cause Andy. Our culture in America is very tough on emotionally sensitive men, routinely discouraging them from expressing their true feelings.

During these early years I began taking Andy to preschool centers where he could play with other children, while the mothers learned more about parenting. Many mothers with first-born children were there, and we shared the same questions. The teachers at the preschool reassured us our children's behavior was normal, and taught us what to expect from the children as they continued to mature. We mothers began to meet outside of class, taking the boys on outings to the park, the zoo, or to our homes. The boys enjoyed the visits and the mothers shared a pleasant time together.

In the meantime, Mike was busy establishing himself professionally. He never came home before 6:30 p.m. and then would eat dinner and study for his Certified Public Accounting exam. One or two evenings a week and some Saturdays he attended review classes at Golden Gate University in preparation for the CPA exam. At home he was always warm and loving with Andy, but was seldom home. I quickly discovered that my role was to do all the parenting of Andy and also take care of Mike. This routine did not sit well with me, but my argument for more of Mike's time for Andy and me fell on deaf ears.

My dream had always been to stay home with my children. My mother always had to work when I was a child. As a youngster, I envied my friends whose mothers were waiting for them when they came home from school. In 1946, divorce was not as acceptable as in today's society. I grew up with the stigma of coming from a 'divorced family'. Already having one failed marriage, my determination was to have a successful second marriage, with a mother who stayed home and cared for the family while the father provided for and loved his family. The problems in my marriage seemed to be my fault. These problems apparently were nonexistent to Mike. Maybe if I could learn to be a better wife and mother, the marriage and Andy would be successful.

The decision not to have any more children was ultimately mine. My hands were full with Andy. The realization came that Mike was not going to be very involved or much help in raising children. In trying to discuss not having more children with Mike, he made clear the fact that he was not willing to have a vasectomy. His reasoning was that if something happened to me, he might want more children in another marriage. Because of the difficulty in giving birth to Andy, my fear was that my next child might have more serious complications in delivery. Mike left the final decision to me and my decision was to have a tubal ligation. The procedure was a simple one and I was home from the hospital the next day.

When Andy was three years old, I decided to return to college part-time and complete the requirements for my teaching credentials. We lived near San Francisco State University and

I applied for entrance into the teachers' certification program, passing the written and oral portions of the entrance exam. An additional requirement was two letters of recommendation which I did not have. Without the letters an applicant could not be admitted to the teaching program. Another factor in my decision not to pursue the application to the program was because Mike and I decided to move to South Bend, Indiana. The story about our move to South Bend will be explained and shared in another chapter.

> *"He had a big heart and was always there for his friends. He lived life on his own terms and showed us all what a true friend should be."*
>
> *'Eulogy: Tim Sundberg'*

*"Pray as if everything depends on you
and work as if everything depends on God."*

St. Ignatius of Loyola

The Statistics

For a moment let me change the focus on the story of Andy's suicide to an analytical perspective. By looking at Andy's suicide as a statistic, how many other adolescents are at risk for suicide or attempted suicide? What is being done to prevent suicide? How many people commit suicide? What age groups are most at risk for suicide? Is there a difference in suicide numbers among ethnic groups? How about differences in the gender of those who attempt or commit suicide? Is a psychiatric disorder necessary to experience a suicidal episode? In this chapter we will attempt to look at the issue of adolescent suicide in this country, and what is being done to address this devastating problem.

Suicide occurs rarely in childhood and early adolescence, but beginning at age 15 the suicide rate increases dramatically. The suicide rate among young people has tripled since the 1950s. Suicide among adolescents in the United States is the third leading cause of death in this age group. The above information is taken from *Adolescence: an Introduction*, by John Santrock, a textbook used in teaching the psychology of adolescence. The same statistics are cited by the American Association of Suicidology.

In May 1994, three months before Andy died, the governor of Arizona established an Adolescent Suicide Task Force. The task force was an outgrowth of the State Select Commission on Adolescent Suicide that originally convened in September 1988. Much of the following information is taken from the *Adolescent Suicide Task Force Report and Recommendations* (ASTFRR) submitted to the Arizona Governor's Office for Children.

In the summer of 1995, a year after Andy's death, the American Association of Suicidology (AAS) held their 28th Conference at the Biltmore hotel in Phoenix. I was still lost in my pain and looking for answers to his suicide and decided to attend the conference. The American Association of Suicidology holds the conference annually in different locations. My hope was that by attending this three-day conference I might find some answers to why my son had committed suicide. This conference was where I first received a copy of the governor's report on adolescent suicide. The report was completed about the time of Andy's death and the statistical facts in the report were very interesting, but disturbing.

A year later I used the information from the ASTFRR report and from the conference to complete a research paper on suicide among Native American youths. The paper was required for a class I was taking in cultural diversity at Ottawa University. My interest in adolescent suicide persuaded me to focus on the unusually high rate of suicide among the Native Americans in Arizona. The rate of suicide among this group of youths is even more horrific than among White youths. Their rate for teen suicide in 1990 was 40.2 deaths per 100,000 population. This rate was more than twice the rate for White teenagers (18.7) and almost nine times the rate for Hispanics (4.6).

An examination of the reasons for the suicides among Native American adolescents found a variety of possible reasons: substandard living conditions, poverty, chronic unemployment, failure at school and poor health. Also the high rate of alcoholism among some tribes is considered a factor. In addition to these reasons and the usual adolescent identity issues young people experience, these young people have a cultural identity to resolve. In an article written in 1992 by John L. McIntosh, he reasons that suicide among Native Americans is committed primarily by the younger population. His explanation for this pattern is the clash of traditional culture with that of the larger Anglo society. Native American adolescents must resolve their conflict in order to perform in a nontraditional society. The results of these conflicts sometimes produce the feeling of belonging to neither culture while being regulated by both.

The following information was obtained from the ASTFRR report. Throughout the decade of the 1980s and the early 1990s, the suicide rate in Arizona has been among the highest in the nation. This is true for adolescents and people of *all* ages in *all* ethnic groups. The National Center for Injury & Control statistics provides two categories for suicide: suicide by firearm, and suicide. Looking at the five states with the highest rates the order is as follows:

Suicide by Firearm - 1995   Suicide - 1995

Rate based on 100,000 per capita

Suicide by Firearm - 1995			Suicide - 1995		
1. Ohio	-	634	1. New York	-	1,370
2. North Carolina	-	609	2. Ohio	-	1,077
3. Arizona	-	546	3. North Carolina	-	908
4. New York	-	522	4. Arizona	-	805
5. Washington	-	455	5. Washington	-	781

From 1985 through 1989, Arizona's rate of suicide for persons of all ages ranked among the five highest states; while the average rate for persons between 15-24 ranked eighth. Researchers found that, "The 1991 Arizona suicide rate was 50.9 percent higher than the national rate, and 58.1 percent higher than the year 2000 national health objective of 10.5 suicides/100,000 population. The suicide rate for individuals 15 through 19 years of age has increased steadily between 1981 and 1991 while the rates for persons 20-24 has declined slightly." (ASTFRR)

According to the AAS the number of suicide *attempts* is three times greater among females than males. But the number of *deaths* is three times higher among males than females. One reason for these differing rates may be the different methods used by men and women: men tend to use more violent methods, such as shooting, stabbing, or hanging themselves, whereas women use less violent methods, such as a drug overdose. Also, according to the AAS, the most common method of suicide is use of firearms: Nationally, 61.1 percent of all suicides in 1990 were firearms related. The second most common method in 1990 was hanging, strangulation or suffocation; ingestion of solid or liquid poisons was the third choice.

In *attempted suicide* the most common method used is an overdose of medication, often in combination with other substances. Other attempts involve jumping from high places, use of cutting instruments such as knives and razors plus hanging, gassing, and traffic accidents. The researchers include traffic accidents in this category, because many experts believe single car accidents are sometimes suicide or attempts. The belief is that the actual attempts and completions are significantly more numerous than reported figures suggest. Many suicidal episodes and actual attempts are never reported. Also, determination of intent is frequently difficult if certain fatalities are planned or accidental, especially those involving motor vehicles.

In the United States the suicide rates seem to differ markedly by ethnic group. The suicide rate of White Americans, 14 per 100,000 persons, is twice as high as that of African Americans and members of other racial groups. The major exception to this pattern is the very high suicide rate of Native Americans as mentioned earlier. Their rate of death in the U.S. is twice the national average.

In May 1998 a Dr. Bell appeared on KAET, Channel 8 in Phoenix to discuss a study he recently concluded of the suicide rate among Black youths. He stated the suicide rate among Black adolescent males increased by 156 percent in the past ten years. Dr. Bell submitted his results in a research article published in the medical community during 1998. My understanding of his comments is that he attributes the increase in Black adolescent suicide to alienation from family and society. He stated that Black youths are beginning to buy into the White society and are losing their sense of ethnic identity.

Statistics taken from the American Association of Suicidology suggest that in western society the elderly are more likely to commit suicide than people in any other age group. More than 21 of every 100,000 persons over the age of 65 in the United States commit suicide. According to several textbooks used in teaching abnormal psychology, some investigators believe that suicide is in fact the leading cause of death among the elderly. The issue of elderly suicide has recently drawn national attention, while the epidemic of suicide among our young has gone unnoticed by our local and state government. Dr. Bell's report on Black adolescent suicide may result in some type of suicide intervention program for Black youth. I do not see the suicide of our youth as a racial issue, but as a common bond, which knows no color and has in common heartbreaking pain for the surviving parents and family.

Some precipitating factors in suicide are stressful events and situations, mood and thought changes, drug and alcohol use, mental disorders and imitation. According to the report by the governor's task force in Arizona, societal stressors such as urbanization, population mobility, poverty, being uneducated, unemployed and disadvantaged members of society are factors. The social factors include the decline in religious/moral values, prevalence of divorce and the startling increase in the number of single-parent families. These societal stressors appear to be associated with feelings of anger, alienation and hopelessness among vulnerable individuals. When associated with psychiatric illness, especially depression, individuals may experience loss of self-esteem, decreased coping skills and a loss of hope. Factors such as the use of alcohol or drugs, the availability of a lethal method (particularly firearms) and the occurrence of stressful life events may increase the likelihood of a suicidal episode.

In a study conducted by Garfinkel, Froese and Hood in 1991 (cited in the ASTFRR) the authors record the rate of suicide in families of adolescent suicide attempters was seven times greater than the rate in families of medical patients. These researchers also found suicidal adolescents are more likely than other adolescents to know someone who has either attempted or committed suicide. In cases involving students who attempted suicide after a friend completed suicide (contagion effect), these studies suggested there was a significant history of psychiatric illness in these children's families.

The most prevalent psychiatric disorders among completed adolescent suicides may be mood disorders, conduct disorder and substance abuse. The ASTFRR report stated that most adolescents committing suicide also had psychological difficulties, experienced long-standing problems in school, and issues with their families and possibly with the law.

In the ASTFRR a study by Kazdin, French, Unis, Esveldt-Dawson and Sherick (1983), found that children who had made a suicide attempt reported more depression and hopelessness than did children who were suicide ideators. Ideation refers to the individual's thoughts of suicide. Hopelessness with depression may be a stronger predictor of suicidal behavior than depression alone.

A shameful or humiliating experience often immediately precipitates completed suicide by the individual. These experiences could be an arrest, perceived failure at school or work, a personal rejection, or interpersonal conflict with a romantic partner or parent. The term *completed suicide* is used to differentiate between those people who attempt suicide and those who complete their suicide. The experience of sexual or physical assault may be a particularly significant risk factor for young women according to the aforementioned task force report.

A general lack of responsible behavior characterizes poor impulse control by adolescents. Particularly, when impulsivity is combined with other risk factors such as depression and substance abuse, the risk of a suicidal episode is greatly increased. Several studies cited in the ASTFRR have found that at least one-third of the adolescents who commit suicide are intoxicated at the time of death and many more may be under the influence of drugs.

Gay youth are two to three times more likely to attempt suicide than other young people (Larkin Street, 1984). While there is nothing inherently self-destructive in homosexual feelings and relationships, suicide attempts by gay and lesbian youth are likely to involve conflicts around sexual orientation. The conflict is because of the overwhelming pressures they face by peer groups in 'coming out' at an early age.

The Arizona task force report stated the rate of suicide by firearms has increased three times faster than the rates of all other methods for 15-19 year olds since 1950. A report from the National Center for Injury Prevention and Control states there were 38,505 firearm-related deaths in the United States in 1994. This number includes 17,866 firearm-related homicides, 18,765 firearm-related suicides, and 1,256 unintentional deaths related to firearms. In a report on firearm related deaths in the U.S. and other countries done by the National Center for Injury Prevention and Control in Atlanta, Georgia the following statistics are disturbing:

1. Among thirty-six countries surveyed, the U.S. is unique in several respects. The U.S. has the highest overall firearm mortality rate, a high proportion of homicides that are the result of firearm injury, and the highest proportion of suicides that result from firearm injury.

   (a) The Arizona task force report also attributes part of the dramatic increase in adolescent suicide to increased pressure by peers, family and school authorities on children to achieve and to be responsible at an early age.

2. The firearm-related suicide rate in the U.S. is five times higher than the rate for other high-income nations and almost seven times higher than the rate for upper-middle-income nations.

   (a) The report recommends more research to identify overall risk factors for firearm-related deaths so that researchers can develop prevention approaches.

Finally, several studies in the task force report have confirmed that suicide rates increase following television or newspaper coverage of suicide (modeling), and that teenagers may be particularly susceptible to this effect. Evidence is unclear as to the how or whether the manner in which the information is presented influences the suicide effect.

The concluding summary of the aforementioned studies on adolescent suicide is:

1. Suicidal behavior is an outcome of psychiatric disorders in combination with exacerbating circumstances.
2. The most common psychiatric disorders associated with suicide are depression, impulse-control disorders and substance abuse.
3. Suicidal behavior is most common among youth with a family history of psychiatric disorders and suicide.
4. Prevention of suicide among adolescents requires the earliest possible identification of psychiatric disorders and initiation of appropriate treatment.
5. Stigmatization surrounding gender identity issues is strongly associated with suicidal behavior.
6. The use of firearms is strongly associated with completed suicides.
7. There is a serious lack of available, accessible and timely services plus inadequate coordination among city, county, state and federal agencies that encounter and intervene in the lives of young people at risk.

In a youth suicide fact sheet compiled in 1997 by the AAS in Washington, DC, the following facts are reported:

1. Suicide ranks as the third leading cause of death for young people (behind only accidents and homicide). For those ages 15-19, suicide is the second leading cause of death.
2. Each year there are approximately 14 suicides for every

100,000 adolescents.

3. Approximately 14 young people between the ages of 15-24 die every day by suicide.

4. Every 1 hr. 40 min. a person under the age of 25 completes suicide.

5. Between the years of 1980-1992, a total of 67,369 persons under the age of 25 completed suicide; accounting for 16.4 % of all suicides.

6. Whereas suicides account for 1.4 % of all deaths in the U.S. annually, they comprise 14 % of all deaths per month among 15-24 year old youths.

7. Over the past 35 years the youth suicide rate has tripled!

8. Suicide rates for 5-19 year olds has increased 28.3 % since 1980. Suicide rates for those between the ages of 10-14 have increased 120 % since 1980.

9. Firearms remain the most commonly used suicide method among youth, despite race or gender, accounting for two of every three completed suicides.

10. Research has shown that access to or the availability of firearms is a significant factor in the increase of youth suicide.

11. As of 1992, the ratios for male to female adolescent suicides were 5:1 for Whites and 7.8:1 for African Americans.

12. Black males (ages 15-19) have shown the largest increase in suicide rates among adolescents. Their suicide rate has increased 165 % since 1980.

13. Research has shown that most adolescent suicides occur in the afternoon or early evening and in their own home.

14. Seven to sixteen percent of adolescents report an incidence of a suicide attempt.

15. Four to eight percent of adolescents report an attempt within the prior twelve months; that is, within a typical

high school classroom, it is likely that three students (one boy and two girls) have attempted suicide in the past year.

16. Fourteen percent of all adolescents have stated on self-report surveys that they have attempted suicide; the true figure may be higher.

17. A prior suicide attempt is an important risk factor for an eventual completion.

18. The typical profile of an adolescent attempter is a female who ingests pills; while the profile of the typical adolescent completer is a male, who dies of a gunshot wound.

19. Not all adolescent attempters may admit to their intent. Therefore, any deliberate self-harming behaviors should be considered serious and in need of further evaluation.

20. The intent of most adolescent attempters seems interpersonal and instrumental. In other words, they want to effect change in the behaviors or attitudes of others.

21. Repeat attempters (those making more than one non-lethal attempt) use their behavior for coping with stress and tend to exhibit more chronic symptomology, poorer coping histories, and a higher presence of suicidal and substance abusive behaviors in their family histories.

22. Up to 60 % of high school students report having suicidal ideation.

Suicidal risk factors for adolescents compiled by the AAS are the following:

1. Presence of a psychiatric disorder (e.g., depression, manic-depression, personality disorders, conduct disorder).

2. Substance abuse or dependency.

3. Expressions/communications of thoughts of suicide, death, dying, or the afterlife (in the context of sadness, boredom, or negative feelings).

4. Poor control over behavior and/or significant change in

an individual's behavior.
5. Impulsive, aggressive behavior, frequent expressions of rage.
6. Previous exposure to their own or others' suicidality.
7. Recent severe stressors.
8. Family loss or instability; significant problems in parental relationships.
9. Difficulties in dealing with sexual orientation; unplanned pregnancy.
10. History of running away or incarceration.

As indicated, many of the statistics cited by the AAS are the same statistics and conclusions reported in the ASTFRR. In an article taken from *Psychology Today* in 1987, Dr. Edwin Shneidman a professor of thanatology at the University of California, Los Angeles and the founder of the American Association of Suicidology found ten common characteristics of suicide. He believes these characteristics form a psychological chart of suicidal terrain. Dr. Shneidman hopes knowledge of this dangerous territory by the public and by mental health professions may be the most effective suicide prevention. Therefore, I am including the ten characteristics he listed in his article.

1. *Unendurable psychological pain.* No one commits suicide out of joy; no suicide is born out of exultation. The enemy to life is pain. Pain is what the suicidal person seeks to escape.

2. *Frustrated psychological needs.* Needs for security, achievement, trust and friendship form much of the landscape of our inner lives. While there are many pointless deaths, there is never a needless suicide. Address these psychological needs, and the suicide will not occur.

3. *The search for a solution.* Suicide is not random; it is

never done pointlessly or without a purpose. It is a way out of a problem, a crisis, an unbearable situation. It may be the only available answer to a real puzzler: "How do I get out of this?"

4. *An attempt to end consciousness.* Suicide is both a movement away from pain and a movement to end consciousness. The aim of suicide is to stop awareness of a painful existence.

5. *Helplessness and hopelessness.* Shame, guilt, loss of effectiveness, frustrated dependency and a host of other feelings have all been proposed as "real" causes of suicide. But underlying all of these is a sense of powerlessness and impotence. The feelings that no one can help with this pain and that there is nothing to do except commit suicide.

6. *Constriction of options.* Instead of looking for a variety of answers for their problems, suicidal individuals think of only two alternatives: a total solution or a total cessation. Desperation and pain have driven all other options out. The most dangerous word in the dictionary of suicide is "only." This word infers the options have been constricted to the single one of death.

7. *Ambivalence.* Some ambivalence is normal. In the typical suicidal state, a person cuts his or her throat and cries out for help at the same time. Both acts are genuine.

8. *Communication of intent.* About 80% of suicidal people give friends and family clear clues about their intention to kill themselves. They give indications of helplessness, make pleas for response and create opportunities for a rescue.

9. *Departure.* Running away from home, quitting a job and abandoning a spouse are all departures, but suicide is the

45

ultimate escape...a plan for a radical, permanent change of scenes.

10. *Lifelong coping patterns.* To spot potential suicides, we must look to previous episodes of disturbance, to the person's way of enduring psychological pain and to a penchant for constricted, "either-or" thinking.

The AAS has compiled the following facts about depression and suicide.

1. Major depression is the psychiatric diagnosis most commonly associated with suicide.

2. About two-thirds of people who complete suicide have a diagnosed depressive disorder at the time of their deaths.

3. Fifteen percent of people who are diagnosed with depression eventually go on to end their lives through suicide.

4. The risk of suicide among people with depression is approximately 30 times that of the general population.

5. Suicide is particularly likely when a depressive episode begins to lift (the person may feel less tension after having made the decision to end their life).

6. People who have had multiple episodes of depression are at greater risk for suicide than those who have had one episode.

7. People who drink alcohol in addition to being depressed are at a greater risk for suicide.

8. People who are depressed and exhibit the following symptoms are at particular risk for suicide:

A. Extreme hopelessness.

B. Lack of interest in activities that were previously pleasurable.

C. Heightened anxiety.

D. Global insomnia.

E. Panic attacks.

F. Delusions or hallucinations.

Combining the reports of the AAS, the ASTFRR and Dr. Shneidman and the many other reports cited here, we find the number of adolescent suicides staggering and increasing. The understanding on suicide among professionals in counseling and psychology is beginning to be understood, but the public is still ignorant of what suicide is all about. One of the problems is the many continued myths held by the general public about suicide. The following myths repeatedly appear in various forms, without accreditation, and are worthy of listing.

The Mythology of Suicide

1. *Myth* - People who talk about killing themselves never commit suicide. *Fact* - Most people who commit suicide have given some clue or warning of their intent; therefore, suicidal threats and attempts should always be treated seriously.

2. *Myth* - The tendency toward suicide is inherited and passed from generation to generation. *Fact* - Although suicide does tend to "run in families," research suggests that suicide is not transmitted genetically.

3. *Myth* - The suicidal person wants to die and feels that there is no turning back. *Fact* - Suicidal people are often ambivalent about dying and frequently will call for help immediately following an attempted suicide.

4. *Myth* - All suicidal people are deeply depressed. *Fact* - Although depression is often associated with suicidal feelings, not all people who kill themselves are obviously depressed. In fact, some suicidal people appear to be happier than they've been in quite a while because they have decided to "resolve" all of their problems at the same time.

47

5. *Myth* - There is a very low correlation between alcoholism and suicide. *Fact* - Alcoholism and suicide often go hand in hand. Alcoholics are prone to suicide and even people who do not normally drink will often ingest alcohol shortly before killing themselves.

6. *Myth* - Suicidal people are mentally ill. *Fact* - Although many suicidal people are depressed and distraught, most of them could not be diagnosed as mentally ill.

7. *Myth* - If someone attempts suicide, they will always entertain thoughts of suicide. *Fact* - Most people who are suicidal are that way for only a very brief period in their lives. If the attempter receives the proper assistance and support, they will probably never be suicidal again. About ten percent of attempters later complete the act.

8. *Myth* - If you ask a person about his suicidal intentions you'll encourage the person to kill himself. *Fact* - Actually, the opposite is true. Asking someone directly about suicidal intent will often lower the anxiety level and act as a deterrent to suicidal behavior by encouraging the ventilation of pent-up emotions.

9. *Myth* - Suicide is quite common among the lower classes. *Fact* - Suicide crosses all socioeconomic groups and no one class is more susceptible to suicide than another.

10. *Myth* - Suicidal people rarely seek medical attention. *Fact* - Research has consistently shown that about 75% of suicidal people will visit a physician within the three months before they kill themselves.

11. *Myth* - Suicide is basically a problem that is limited to young people. *Fact* - Suicide rates rise with age and reach their peak among older White males.

12. *Myth* - Professional people do not kill themselves. Fact - Physicians, lawyers, dentists and pharmacists appear to

have high suicide rates.

13. *Myth* - When a depression lifts, there is no longer any danger of suicide. *Fact* - The greatest danger of suicide exists during the first three months after a person recovers from a deep depression.

14. *Myth* - Suicide is a spontaneous activity that occurs without warning. *Fact* - Most suicidal people plan their self-destruction in advance and then present clues indicating that they have become suicidal.

15. *Myth* - Because it includes the Christmas season, December has a high suicide rate. *Fact* - There is not a rash of suicides at Christmas, and December has the lowest suicide rate of any month. The rate is highest from March to May; Spring has the greatest admission rate to hospitals.

Five years have passed since my son's death and an increasing number of adolescents have committed suicide; still, no city, state or federal government agency has created an agenda to prevent the continuing loss of our youth. Why! In my opinion, the reason is that adolescents do not vote, therefore they have no political presence. Without political advocacy, there can be no funding for programs to prevent suicide among adolescents. These statements may sound simplistic, but without funding there can be no programs; without programs there can be no prevention or reduction in the suicide rate among adolescents. One does not have to be Albert Einstein to figure out this equation. I realize even with the best of programs there will be suicides, but maybe, just maybe, we could save a few youths, and save a few families from the devastating loss of a child.

Are our children not worth the money, time and effort to be included on a political agenda? Our children are our future—without them, we have no future. My son is dead, and I have no future. Does this sound dramatic, traumatic? The truth often is. How does one build a future from ashes? Maybe, by helping responsible adults become aware of this suicide epidemic among our youth. And encouraging the adults to pick up the banner and join together to fight for the lives of our children.

> *Risk factors that describe Andy :*
> "*Suicidal ideation.*
> *Depression and hopelessness.*
> *Poor impulse control.*
> *Under the influence of alcohol.*
> *Stressful life events and humiliating experiences.*
> *Disturbed interpersonal relationships.*
> *Accessibility of firearms.*"

> *'Observation': JG*

[4]

The Move to South Bend

To return to the story, while Mike and I were living in San Francisco we were searching for a more personal relationship with God. We attended various Catholic churches, trying to find a church congregation that met our spiritual needs. Actually, I was the problem, having never been raised in any particular religion. As a youth my friends were Catholic, Baptist, and other denominations. At the age of seventeen my conclusion was that God did not exist: this thinking undoubtedly was a result of my negative experiences with formal religion as a child. Although, with maturity and experience my wonder at the creation of life made me realize there must be a God. In my mind the miracle of the birth of a child could not be an accident created by nature.

Mike, baptized at birth, was a devout Catholic and never put any pressure on me to become a member of his faith. When we decided to be married I volunteered to study Catholicism and join the Catholic church. My mixed-up religious experiences as a child made me question and challenge some doctrines in the Catholic church. Mike was very patient with me, but since he accepted the church without question, could not answer my doubts. This difference led us to seek answers

51

from those in the church who could explain my questions. In our search for a more compatible doctrine we began attending Catholic 'charismatic' meetings. Mike and I felt we had finally found our place. These people were friendly, loving and full of the love of God. They invited us to join their small growing community in San Francisco. Mike and I went to our parish church on Sundays, and then would attend their prayer meetings and small prayer group sessions during the week. The leaders taught men to love and honor their wives, and the men treated the women with love and respect. The same leaders taught the women to honor and love their husbands, and cherish their children. These were the same tenets we believed and valued. In 1977 more Catholic charismatic groups were developing in other states. The charismatic leaders in San Francisco said they believed God was calling them to move to a small covenant commune in South Bend, Indiana.

Andy would be four years old in July, and we were concerned about raising him in a big city without friends or family. Mike and I talked about making the move to South Bend, and what we wanted for our lives. We were ready to make a change. The move to Indiana would be made with seventy other members of the charismatic group.

The group arrived in South Bend on a hot steamy July afternoon in 1977. The temperature was ninety-eight degrees, and the humidity was ninety-eight percent. South Bend is a lovely, lush green college town known for housing Notre Dame University on the banks of the St. Joseph River. After we decided to move to South Bend, I flew there a few months prior to the move to look for a house to buy. My successful purchase of our home in San Francisco convinced Mike to trust me in making another wise choice in South Bend. Success, again. The house was located near an old apple orchard north of

Notre Dame. This was to be the nicest home we would ever own, although we did not know that at the time.

On the day of the move from San Francisco to South Bend we drove from very early in the morning until midday when we stopped to rest. We formed a caravan with several other families that were also making the move. The trip was our first vacation since Andy was born. Andy's birthday was July 19, and we arrived in South Bend on July 1, 1977. Andy was a good traveler, sleeping in the morning, and playing quietly with his toys in the back seat of the car. At the end of each day we would stop, making sure to stay at a motel that had a swimming pool. After checking into the motel, Mike, Andy and I would go to the pool and cool off by swimming and playing games in the water. The trip for Andy was an exciting and fun adventure.

In South Bend, Mike was very pleased with the house and the location. Andy being his usual happy self was enjoying the friends he made in the neighborhood, and within the covenant community. The three of us were very busy. Mike had to find a job, and I was busy getting unpacked and settled. The community welcomed us lovingly and kept us busy attending prayer meetings and community service activities.

A month after we were settled in our new home in the covenant community, a woman who was director of a Montessori preschool invited me to work with her at the school. Andy had been in preschool the year before in San Francisco, and my thought was teaching in a preschool would work well for Andy and me. The position was part-time, allowing me to be with Andy while he was in preschool and also earn a little extra money. The decision to work in the preschool turned out to be a mistake. The director was experiencing emotional problems and I found the work, and being supportive of her, both physically and emotionally exhausting. Andy liked preschool, although he seemed to have some difficulty staying on task in certain activities. Playing was Andy's favorite activity. He did not take to the Montessori reading activities at all. He could recite his alphabet, and was very articulate. Andy's vocabulary was extensive. Mike or I read to him every night and his memory for these stories was exceptional. He liked to count, and knew his colors, and other basics, but seemed indifferent to reading. Andy had many friends to play with, and I would baby-sit other boys near his age in the covenant community; the mothers took turns baby-sitting the children. This plan allowed the mothers a pleasant break in the day from their children. Women in the community were encouraged to help each other and give spiritual and emotional support to the families.

The Catholic charismatic movement is a very fundamental religious movement begun in response to the impersonal formal atmosphere many parishes felt existed in the Catholic church. The people attracted to the charismatic movement felt a need for a more personal relationship with God than offered by traditional parishes. The charismatic movement reminded me of some Pentecostal meetings I attended in my youth. The leaders in the Catholic charismatic movement conducted 'Life in the Spirit' seminars, where people prayed over members to receive the gifts of the Holy Spirit.

Within a few months I realized the biased attitude of the leaders toward the role of women in the community caused me difficulty in adjusting to the mentality and lifestyle of the community. The attitude seemed to be that a woman should stay at home, subjugate herself to the husband and to the movement, and her children. I was suffering from culture shock; the people in the Midwest tend to be more traditional in their view of family and the role of the woman in the home. Having been born and raised in California by a divorced mother, my view of the role of a woman in society was different. I had been self-supporting for more than fifteen years, and thought of myself as intelligent, capable of making decisions and equal to men. In addition, my belief was that women were the caretakers of the home and the primary nurturer of the children, although a man should share in the responsibilities of raising the children and caring for the home.

In this community a woman's place was definitely in the home. Her identity was through her husband and her children. Her function was to serve her husband, family and community. A woman's husband was her head, and superior to her. The husband was second only to God in importance to a woman's life. I tried very hard to make myself fit the desired mold of the covenant, believing my selfishness and lack of faith was preventing me from accepting my role. The experience was similar to becoming a character out of the *Stepford Wives*, a science fiction novel about husbands who turned their imperfect wives into perfect wives by changing them into very feminine, docile, mechanical robots.

Mike had some difficulty finding a position as a certified public accountant in South Bend. After a month of interviewing he was offered employment with a CPA firm in Plymouth, a small town located sixty miles south of South Bend.

At this juncture, my life consisted of working part-time in the Montessori preschool and participating in covenant community life. Andy was happily adjusting, enjoying the change of seasons and our huge backyard.

Because of my childhood experiences with animals, I thought a pet would be good for Andy. He loved animals and I was raised around cats and dogs and parakeets. My father in

Arkansas had goats the children played with, and there were always cows, chickens and pigs on the farm where he lived. When Andy was a baby in San Francisco we adopted Uriah, a cocker spaniel mix. She was a lovable dog, but not too bright and she followed Andy everywhere. We decided not to take Uriah with us on the trip to South Bend, and gave her to a family in San Francisco.

In South Bend we located a black Labrador puppy, Boots, who turned out to be a nightmare. As she grew older she would constantly jump the backyard fence, or dig holes in the backyard. The dog even had a nervous breakdown. Once after she jumped the fence while in heat she disappeared. Two months later she showed up at our front door. The poor animal was skin and bones. Someone had tied her up and starved her. She had rope burns around her neck where she had been tied and shook and quivered when anyone came near her. Someone had completely cowed her, but she managed to get loose and find her way home. The cruelty of some people to animals is criminal. Also, she was pregnant when she arrived at our door. In spite of the period of abuse she never growled or became mean. Andy, Boots, and I often went for peaceful walks in the old apple orchard, just a few yards from our home.

South Bend had a record-breaking snowfall that year, 1977, one hundred seventy-seven inches. To my knowledge South Bend has not had this much snow since we moved to Phoenix. We did not see the ground for five months because of the snow. One snowstorm was so severe we were snowed in for five days before the snowplow could dig us out. Fortunately, Mike was snowed in with us at home. Some men were stranded at their offices and away from their families for the five days. On the day the storm hit, Mike's truck stalled in the driveway and he was unable to drive to work. The incident was a blessing for us. The three of us were forced to spend time together, because there was nothing else to do. We could not go anywhere, and no one could come to us. Fortunately, I had purchased groceries the day before the storm hit, so the cupboards were full and we ate well. Andy had fun playing in the snowdrifts and building igloos while Mike and I shoveled the snow off the driveway. The three of us enjoyed the food, the warmth and closeness. The five days we were snowed in is probably the nicest memory we have of our stay in South Bend. We were a family spending time together. Mike did not have anything else to do but play with Andy and keep me company.

By the middle of April, South Bend had five months of snow on the ground. We were desperate for outdoor activity without the snow and slush. One day Mike decided he wanted to barbeque and he set up the hibachi grill in the backyard with snow still packed three feet high around him. The barbeque was a success. After the snowplow shoveled us out from the storm, Mike returned to working his fifty-five hours a week, and attending his community activities. The cold and snow prevented Andy from playing outside very much. He began to watch more television than I preferred. Mike never noticed the behavior, seeming content in his work and community services. I finally summoned the courage to tell him I could no longer live in South Bend or with the community. Mike confided that he, too, was disappointed with the community demands and lifestyle and was ready to move. He agreed that his family came first and that we would move from South Bend as a family.

We decided to move to Phoenix. The cost of living in San Francisco was extremely expensive, and we had already sold our home there. Mike's family lived in Phoenix and we decided we wanted to be near his family. In July 1978, exactly one year after arriving in South Bend we moved to Phoenix.

As we were preparing to move we realized that Boots could not make the trip with us. We took her and her puppy to the animal shelter. Taking them to the shelter broke my heart, but there was no other reasonable choice. We could not find a home for her or the puppy before we left South Bend. After explaining the facts to Andy, he accepted the situation about the pets.

The community in South Bend was disappointed to see us leave, but we parted on good terms. We have stayed in touch over the years with a few of the families who moved with us from San Francisco and remained in South Bend. Some families, like us, could not adjust to the lifestyle in South Bend and relocated elsewhere. The people in community were very nice and the concept and the personal support they offer one another is wonderful. Emotionally, I simply could not deal with some of the religious beliefs. There is a charismatic group in Tempe and we attended some of their prayer meetings. We enjoyed the prayer time and the fellowship, but had no intention of joining community. Although, the charismatic group in Tempe is less structured than in South Bend, allowing members to have time for a life outside of community as well as involvement in religious activities.

Mike's family was thrilled to have us move to Phoenix, and we stayed with his parents while we looked for a house to buy. On August 1, 1978, we moved into our current home and took up residence. The house was an older home in a nice neighborhood in an area where the school district had an excellent reputation.

Andy turned five in July while we were in South Bend. He was a bright, cheerful and loving child. In our new home in

Phoenix we enjoyed watching him play in the backyard. He never seemed to mind playing alone. After playing games with him we would go to McDonald's, but when we were busy, he never complained. Andy had a wonderful imagination, and could entertain himself for hours. Andy quickly made friends with the other children in the neighborhood, especially a family with three boys, two of whom were close to his age.

Once again, Mike did not have time to spend with Andy. He was too busy becoming established in business. Andy never complained about his daddy not being there for him. My pleas to Mike to spend time with Andy fell on deaf ears. Mike was doing what his father before him had done, provide a living for his family. That was his job, and mine was to take care of Andy, the home, and him. Mike continued to work long hours, and I increased the drinking that started on arrival in South Bend.

Andy wanted another dog, but Mike set his foot down. He did not care for dogs, and especially not one in the house. So Andy and I went to the animal shelter to find a kitten. I had never cared much for cats since a cat had scratched my little sister and she died of an infection. I thought we would find a kitten, but the day we went to the shelter we did not find one we wanted to take home. We saw many adult cats in cages. Some of the adult cats would hiss and strike out, others would simply meow pitifully. As we looked at the cats, one cat put her paw gently through the bars of the cage and drew Andy's finger toward her, without scratching him. An attendant gave us permission to take this cat out of her cage. The cat was very gentle. I handed her to Andy, and she put both paws around his neck and purred into his ear. Her behavior made Andy fall in love with her immediately. I tried to talk him out of choosing her and to wait for a kitten, but he would not let her go and she would not let go of Andy.

Fuzzy was a long-haired cat, soft and gentle as a lamb. She was about a year old when we adopted her, and whoever owned her before had obviously loved her. She was a 'people cat', and she loved being around people, especially children. She carried herself with majesty, her long tail up in the air gently making her presence known. In the twenty years she lived with us she never scratched anyone, not even accidentally. Andy would lug her around everywhere he went. She was his doll. He would dress her up in clothes, putting a Snoopy hat and goggles from the Red Baron days on her. She would simply sit quietly and let him dress her. We have a photograph of Fuzzy wearing a matador hat and another picture with sunglasses on, all things she wore for Andy.

Fuzzy had one litter of kittens before being spayed. She gave birth on the twin bed across from Andy's bed. Andy came to our room early one morning, and with his eyes wide in amazement told us Fuzzy was having babies. We watched as she gave birth to the kittens. We were surprised she did not try to hide somewhere to have the kittens. We thought that cats gave birth where no one could find their babies. She gave birth to four adorable kittens. After the kittens were a week old and started moving around, we moved them and Fuzzy from the bed to the closet floor in Andy's room. We were afraid the kittens would fall off the bed. Many mornings Andy could be found with his legs sticking out of the closet, while he sat in the closet holding the four kittens as Fuzzy watched peacefully. We enjoyed many hours watching the kittens play and grow. There are many pictures of the kittens playing king of the mountain on a cat pole platform, and chasing each other through Andy's *Fisher Price* parking garage. When the time came we found good homes for the kittens.

Fuzzy was always there for Andy throughout his entire life. She slept on his bed, cuddling up in his arms when he wanted to hold her. Later she even shared Andy's bed with Gage, my cocker spaniel, although she quickly let Gage know who was boss.

Andy started kindergarten in August 1978, having just turned five years old. I realize now starting him early was a mistake. In my mind there was no hurry for him to start school, but he was so verbal and knew the fundamentals that perhaps starting school would be in his best interest. He was such a friendly child we thought school would be good for him socially; meeting other children and having playmates. When the school staff pretested him for school they reported he tested in the average range for preparedness. They said he could either start now or wait a year because his birth date was in July. After discussing the issue with Mike, we decided to have Andy start kindergarten at age five.

His kindergarten teacher was an older man who wore a patch over one eye. He seemed nice enough, but we found out later that he yelled at the children, and threw erasers at them. In the class, Andy 'learned' the alphabet and numbers, which surprised me, because he already knew them. He did not excel in school academics, preferring to socialize with his friends, and daydream. This behavior was to remain a consistent pattern throughout his school years.

Andy continued to attend public school through the second grade. Each year we became more disillusioned with the public school system. He was labeled by the teachers as bright and immature; an underachiever by the ripe old age of seven... a sad commentary.

I agree with several educators who have said 'it is not the children who fail, but the schools who fail the children'. As parents, we give the schools our best and our brightest children, and the schools fail to ignite the natural desire to learn that is present in all children when they first enter school.

> *"Once, parents were given all the credit and all the blame–for how their children turned out. Then researchers told us that heredity determines who we are. Now the way heredity shapes who we are is found to be less like one-way dictation and more like spirited rounds of call and response."*
>
> *'Psychology Today 1997'*

[5]

St. Francis Xavier Elementary

At this stage of Andy's development, Mike and I considered that his social and moral growth, as well as his academic performance, would benefit by attending a parochial school which offered a more personal value system. Perhaps this decision was based partially on the fact that Mike had attended parochial school.

St. Francis Xavier Elementary School was originally founded in 1927. The Blessed Virgin Mary order of nuns initially taught the children who attended St. Francis. The school has an excellent academic reputation, and many graduates from St. Francis go to either Xavier High School or Brophy College Preparatory. Both high schools are located practically next door to St. Francis. In past years, Xavier High was an all female school and Brophy was an all male school. Both schools have outstanding academic records. Many parents who can afford the tuition send their children to these high schools in preparation for college.

As a point of interest, today, the religious orders are not attracting as many young people to teaching religious vocations. Perhaps, because the young adults are not willing to lead such a structured life. The result from the decline in novitiates entering the religious orders has caused many convents in the United States to close. As an example, the Blessed Virgin Mary order of nuns has a residence directly behind St. Francis Xavier school and has only elderly nuns in residence. A result of the loss of nuns is that lay teachers now teach at St. Francis. When Andy attended St. Francis only one nun was working at the school, and she worked in the library. The nun who had been principal when I first visited St. Francis in 1981 was no longer there by the time Andy started school in the Fall.

Andy started school at St. Francis in third grade. At St. Francis the children learn cursive writing in second grade and in public school the children do not begin cursive writing until third grade. Because he had attended public school, this meant that Andy would start St. Francis with writing skills behind the other children. When the principal was questioned about Andy repeating second grade, she said he would be all right in third grade. My thought was that he would fare better by repeating second grade.

This decision was the beginning of the downward spiral of education for Andy. If I had gone with my intuition who knows how the future might have been changed. Instead, I continued to believe that others knew what was best for my son. This pattern of my behavior continued until he died. I learned, too late, that my insight was correct and the others had been terribly wrong. There is no consolation in this reality.

To make matters worse for Andy, his teacher's method of teaching was to scare the children into learning. Andy, being a very sensitive child, responded to her style of teaching by shutting down and throwing up. The pattern of stomach problems, vomiting, and using every trick known to kids to avoid going to school became common for him. His sensitive stomach from infancy continued and whenever he was upset he would vomit.

After Andy began parochial school in September my doctor diagnosed me with breast cancer. One of the mothers whose children attended St. Francis volunteered to take Andy to and from school while I was recovering from surgery. She was pleasant, but not the warm comforting type. Her own children were painfully shy, and they were not much support for Andy either. Andy never overtly complained but he continued to exhibit symptoms of stress. Obviously, Mike was now worried about me and also concerned about his career. I had always taken care of Mike and Andy, and Mike was lost without me home to make sure his world went smoothly. The doctors jokingly said that they thought Mike would have to be put in the bed beside me when they told him of my breast cancer.

While in the hospital my worry was about Andy, but he seemed to do fine without me at home to take care of him. Mike and Andy survived with the help of neighbors. The medical staff did not allow Andy to visit me in the hospital because he was too young. My stay in the hospital was for a week and this was the first time for me to be away from Andy.

Initially, I had gone into outpatient surgery to have a benign lump removed and on regaining consciousness the doctor informed me the lump was malignant. While in the hospital, my difficulty was in deciding whether to allow the doctors to remove my breast. The decision may not seem like a big deal, considering the alternative, but death has never held any fear for me. Besides, since our society is so image conscious and I had always felt good about my figure, I was reluctant to agree to the surgery. My breasts were not anything special, but they were mine and in my mind part of my image as a desirable woman. Several doctors and nurses were pressuring me to have the mastectomy. During prayer one night my feeling was that God was telling me to live to see Andy grown. Andy needed me, and he was more important than a breast, so permission was given to have a modified radical mastectomy.

Unfortunately, after the surgery I became obsessed with a need to live my remaining life fully. I became as driven as Mike to succeed, returning to graduate school in addition to qualifying for sales licenses in real estate and life insurance. Mike had convinced me I would make a good salesperson, because of my rapport with people. The truth is I was terrible at sales, being unable to persuade people to buy a house or insurance. These career pursuits were a waste of time and energy, with me running in circles trying to decide what career to pursue. During all these distractions my goal was still to be a perfect wife and mother.

A neighbor took care of Andy while I worked part-time, and this was probably another mistake. Andy's sensitivity needed someone who could be calm and firm with him. The neighbor was a very nice person, but a very high-strung woman who yelled at the children continuously. Of course, these choices and incidents are clearer in hindsight. At the time I was so wrapped up in trying to make something of myself, and failing miserably, that I could not see the obvious. The obvious was Andy developing a dislike for school and he needed help. He was not doing well in class, although his teachers told me he was bright and simply a daydreamer. As a mother, I knew he was intelligent but not motivated. He loved for me to read to him but had difficulty learning to read himself.

Everyone, teachers, principal, other parents told me he was just not focused and spoiled because he was an only child. We tried every suggestion to encourage his motivation but with little success. Being unable to say 'no' and set firm boundaries with Andy made me inconsistent in disciplining him. Loving him desperately, my difficulty was in requiring behavior that made him unhappy or angry. He was such a beautiful child, with bright blue eyes, curly hair and a winning smile that saying 'no' to him was hard for anyone. He learned early simply to bat the baby blues, smile, and he would probably get whatever he wanted. He was never hateful or sassy with his teachers and only got in trouble for not paying attention. Andy was even an altar boy at the church, helping the priests serve mass on Sundays.

As a father, Mike exhibited little patience in playing with or teaching Andy. Mike's father had been very authoritarian, spanking the children when he felt they needed disciplining. Mike was not into spanking but wanted Andy to obey his elders. Mike's lack of patience with Andy made me hesitate to have him involved in the discipline of Andy. Mike was never home before 6:30 p.m. and worked all day Saturdays, making him an absentee father; an early point of friction in our parenting. My desire was for Mike to be actively involved with Andy, doing father-son projects. Mike, on the other hand, never wanted to do any activity without me. From the time Andy was five Mike rarely played ball with him or taught him other little boy games without me first becoming angry about his apparent lack of attention. After years of trying to make Mike into the kind of father I thought he should be, I gave up and accepted Mike as he was. I tried to take Mike's role as a father, but could not be a male and relate to my son in ways only males can relate to males. A boy needs his father involved with him in activities, which are predominantly male-oriented. The myth that mothers can be a father and a mother to a child is a lie.

When Andy was about two years old, the song, *Cat's in a Cradle*, became popular. The first time I heard the song I cried, because the words reflected what was happening to

Mike and Andy. Interestingly, more than fifteen years later a therapist would play Mike this song and he failed to recognize the parallel to his own family. This incident occurred less than four years before Andy died. Mike's idea that he would 'someday have a relationship' with Andy would never become a reality. The statement 'someday Andy and I will be close' was Mike's pat answer whenever I tried to convince him to be more involved with Andy. My response to Mike was always, 'What makes you think there will be a someday?' Again I was right, but being right does not always resolve an issue.

As a matter of routine Andy was always easy to manage. His babysitters never had any problems with him. He liked to play games and listen to stories. He went to bed by nine o'clock in the evening without complaint. In truth, Andy went to bed without being told. He always needed many hours of sleep. We continued to read to him most nights but he was never interested in reading for himself. One thing we observed when he was a baby was his lack of initiative. Andy was always willing to allow someone else to do a task for him. However, he did not seem to like having attention focused on him in school, as some children. Andy never appeared shy but simply never put himself forward as a leader. He would never assert himself and would allow other boys to push him around. A pattern of passive behavior continued for Andy until he reached adolescence. Sometimes the other boys were mean, but Andy was fun and used humor to make the other children like him.

Andy made many long-term friends at St. Francis. Often I felt guilty because Andy was an only child and obviously the center of my attention. Maybe my reaction was to overcompensate by inviting other children over to visit and spend the weekend; this pattern began early in his life and continued until he took charge of selecting his friends. The exact order of friends is vague, but Richard, a classmate, became Andy's closest friend. He, too, was an only child and they shared an interest in *Star Wars* and *G.I. Joe*. Andy developed a fascination with guns when he was young, although we never encouraged the interest. I dislike guns, but owned a small handgun purchased in Fresno after my divorce. Andy never saw the gun until he was grown. Mike never had any interest in guns, yet from infancy Andy was pointing his finger and saying "pow, pow." These games were an extension of the old 'cowboys and Indians'.

Richard and Andy spent a great deal of time together. Richard's parents indulged Richard more than I indulged Andy; nevertheless, Richard's mother made him study and do well in school. If he had homework he could not come over until his homework was completed. In trying this method with Andy he would simply wait me out until bedtime. He had very passive-resistant behavior, defined as when a person does not argue with you, but does not comply either. My guess is that another description could be stubborn. Me, I was passive-aggressive; accepting slights, abuses and neglect until I eventually exploded. Andy once made a card for me in school that read, "I love my mom, but I wish she would not get so mad." Until receiving that card, I did not realize my anger was so apparent.

Another complication was emerging, I was drinking heavily at the time for a number of reasons. My marriage was not turning out as planned, and I did not know how to make our lives better. Although divorce was now more widely accepted than when I was a child, my wish was that Andy not experience the trauma of divorce. Another fear was about my ability to support Andy and myself. These fears along with my other fears of inadequacy kept me in my marriage. My decision was to see a marriage counselor and talking to her allowed me to examine my feelings. When the therapist suggested divorce I stopped seeing her. My pattern of changing counselors whenever they suggested divorce continued over the years. My wish was for help making my marriage work, not a divorce. Maybe divorce might have changed the outcome. Maybe not. My husband is a good man, and he was doing the best he could. He did not know how to be a husband or father any better than I knew how to be a wife and mother.

In the meantime, we involved Andy in activities such as soccer, T-ball and Little League. He exhibited no interest in sports, a big disappointment to his father who loved sports. Andy tried Cub Scouts, but did not continue because a male troop leader could not be found to guide the boys. At the time a woman could not be a troop leader in the Cub Scouts.

As rationale for Andy's problems I have often reasoned that he was left-handed and we live in a right-handed world. Maybe, being left-handed made life twice as difficult for him; because teachers and coaches were always teaching him to be right-handed. Andy learned to write left-handed but in baseball he batted right-handed. We found out later from one of his friends that Andy fired a gun with his left hand. The night he died the gun was in his right hand and the wound to his right temple.

A few months after my mastectomy, my mother died suddenly and I had to go to California to take care of my stepfather and my siblings, and plan my mother's burial. My mother died from a brain aneurism. Her heart was failing, and her health had been deteriorating dramatically for several years. On several occasions my mother told me she wanted to go quickly, and she did. Of course, to lose her was sad, but I was at peace with her death knowing she had lived life on her terms.

A month after my mother's death, and after returning to Phoenix, I started a full-time job as corrections officer in the women's prison on Van Buren Street. My duty shift was at night and five weeks later I quit. My emotional and physical stress in the previous months was taking a toll and I could not tolerate the hours or the work. Working as a corrections officer was an education in reality, but my tender spirit could not handle working in the emotionally depressing and physically demanding environment. Staying home with Andy was a better decision, because I was in control of Andy and our lifestyle.

One morning when going to bed after working the night shift at the prison, Andy came to my bedroom door with tears in his eyes. He explained to me he had lied to his teacher about his lack of religious instruction prior to communion. I told him not to worry that I would talk to his teacher about the incident.

After Andy left for school, I called his third-grade teacher and explained what Andy had done. The problem was Andy had not received the religious preparation necessary before receiving communion. The teacher laughed and said Andy's receiving communion was not a big deal. She said something like 'no harm done, and God did not strike him dead'. I was shocked by Andy's deceit. This was the first time that my darling child had deliberately lied.

My response was to tell his father, and I did; we decided to calmly ask Andy about the incident. I can still remember his face when he knew his behavior had been discussed, his eyes became even larger and rounder and filled with tears, his lower lip quivering. He had simply wanted to taste the wafer given in communion. We explained that lying was wrong and that we had been looking forward to celebrating his first communion by being at church with him, and later having a party to celebrate. We told him the consequences for his actions would be that he would not have the party. He accepted the punishment without complaint. Staying upset with a child that is so easily disciplined is very difficult.

The third-grade teacher advanced Andy to fourth grade although she complained that he was very immature. The fourth grade was team taught, and within a few weeks two frantic teachers were literally yelling that Andy was not ready for fourth grade. He was too immature and should have been retained in third grade. The teachers held meetings with the principal, Mike and me: they stated the embarrassment would be too traumatic for Andy to repeat third grade at St. Francis, and we should send him elsewhere. We did not want him back in the public school system because we felt public school education was inferior to parochial school instruction.

Another parochial school, St. Thomas, was filled and with a waiting list. What were we to do? Public school was not an option. Finally, I talked to the principal at St. Francis and told him my dilemma. He was a new principal at the school that year, and was kind and caring. After talking with another third-grade teacher we decided that Andy would stay at St. Francis, and repeat third grade, but with a different teacher. The new teacher was calm and loving and handled the situation with Andy very professionally. We explained the transfer to Andy as best we could, stating that the teachers and his parents had made a mistake by advancing him to fourth grade. Again, he accepted the change without complaint, made confident by receiving the kindness and patience he needed from the teacher and parents.

In the third-grade class Andy met and developed friendships that lasted until the time of his death. These friendships are what made me keep Andy at St. Francis, even as time began to show he was not faring well in his classes. Several years before his repeating third grade I suspected Andy had a learning disability, but did not know enough about the condition to pursue testing. In discussion with the teachers they had told me 'no', Andy was simply immature. Andy struggled through fourth grade, where the emphasis was on academics and homework every night. In fifth grade Andy had a delightful teacher who seemed able to inspire the best effort from him. He actually enjoyed school and his grades were above average. She found nothing wrong with Andy intellectually or emotionally, other than the fact he was a little boy who liked playing more than school work. She did not think his behavior was abnormal. The children in her class loved her as much as she loved them. Unfortunately for St. Francis, this exceptional teacher left for the public school sector where she could earn more money.

When Andy was about ten years old, he expressed an interest in Tae Kwon Do, a martial art. My thought was that this physical commitment would be good discipline for him since he had no interest in sports. I tried to talk Mike into joining Andy at the gym, a male bonding sort of pursuit. Mike would not consider being involved in martial arts unless the entire family participated. I did not really have an interest in martial arts, but felt the skill and experience would be good for Andy. We continued in the program for over a year until I quit because of the reconstructive surgery for my breast. Mike also stopped. Andy did not want to continue alone and that was the end of Tae Kwon Do.

At St. Francis, the junior high school curriculum began with sixth grade. The purpose behind the program was to give the children an extra year to adjust to moving to a variety of classrooms, and having seven different teachers. This process sounds logical, but not when one or more of those teachers are 'Attila the Hun'. There was at least one junior high teacher that made Andy's third-grade teacher seem like a lamb. There were a few other teachers that Andy did not do well with, either. The headaches and vomiting and trips to the nurse returned with a vengeance. He would do anything to avoid going to school. To add to the problem, Andy did have bronchial problems that made him susceptible to colds and flu. These illnesses caused him to miss more school than we wanted to accept. One doctor asked me if Andy had asthma, and my reply was 'no', but now I wonder because he had so many respiratory problems. Andy began gaining weight. He had always been a picky eater and skinny. Now he found fast food, which was high in fat content and he loved hamburgers. Since he did not like walking, a hobby Mike and I enjoyed, his only exercise was playing with friends.

In 1984 when we could afford a vacation we started renting a house for a week in Mission Beach, California. The first time the three of us went Andy was alone much of the time, my feeling was that he should have company. At this time he was in third grade and very young. Later, we began to take Andy's cousins, who were close to his age, and one year we brought his friend Richard. These guests gave Andy someone to play with while Mike and I swam in the surf, relaxed and read on the beach. We did take the kids to Sea World, and a few other places, but Mike liked to rest and vegetate on his vacation. When we first started going to Mission Beach, I tried to get Mike to do more sightseeing. I was never very good at persuading him into activities, and as usual, eventually gave up. Andy, on the other hand, loved to play games outdoors. Reading was his least favorite activity.

While all this confusion was going on at home I was working full-time at one job or another; changing jobs three times in five years and finally teaching at St. Francis for two years during Andy's sixth and seventh grade years. I tried not to interfere with Andy's teachers, probably to his detriment. My intent was not to be an overly protective mother, or an interfering one. We had plenty of those at St. Francis, and my determination was not to abuse my position as a teacher to seek favors or special treatment for Andy.

Andy was struggling academically, refusing to apply himself to school. I tried encouraging him, but with little success, and Mike did not know what to do either. Mike relied on me to know how to raise Andy. The principal's wife was a special education reading teacher and we decided to ask her to come to our home and evaluate him. She found nothing wrong with his reading ability; he read slowly, but his comprehension was excellent. His memory was always outstanding. If he heard something once, he would remember whatever he heard. I remember helping him review for his final exam in history in the eighth grade, reading him the questions and him giving me the correct answer the first time. He received 100 percent on his final, but a 'C' in the course, because of not turning in homework. This, too, was to be a pattern throughout school: ace the test, but get a poor grade because he refused to do homework. The refusal was covert, of course. He just never brought the assignment home, or lied and told me he had done the work, or that he had no homework. The consequence of Andy's behavior was me yelling, threatening to cut privileges, but usually giving in.

Mike and I did not believe in corporal punishment, except under dire circumstances. I think Andy was spanked once on the bottom by me when he was two years old after he ran into the street, because I was afraid he might be killed. His father only spanked him about three times that I can remember. Then the swat was carefully on the bottom, and never in anger. These 'blows' from his father were apparently traumatic to both of them. Later when Andy was in high school, he told some of his friends that his father beat him. Nothing could be further from the truth. My guess is that spanking Andy truly hurt Mike more than Andy. Later, thanks to a good therapist, I realized Mike was as big a softy as me. Therefore, he let me take the responsibility for discipline, so he did not have to be the bad guy.

In consideration for Andy's welfare I asked him if my teaching at St. Francis bothered him, and he said my being there at the school did make him uneasy. He was a student in my sixth and seventh grade classes. I never singled him out for attention and he never tried to take advantage of the fact that I was his mother. For me, teaching junior high was very stressful and I decided to try my hand at teaching at the community college level. I loved teaching and loved young people, but my level of tolerance for stress was not very high. The duty of teaching and trying to be a good wife and mother was grueling.

Also, I was beginning to address my drinking problem and trying to change my behavior. My husband was oblivious to the fact that I drank too much until I drew my drinking to his attention. Mike had difficulty believing my drinking was interfering with my ability to be an effective wife and mother. Mike prefers to see only the good in people, especially those he loves. I never went into clinical treatment, but did attend Alcoholics Anonymous meetings off and on for years. Most of my drinking was done at home and never went beyond drinking in the evenings at the end of the day. I think some people at the AA meetings did not think I really fit the 'alcoholic' profile. I asked several women to be my sponsors, but could never get anyone to work with me. At an AA meeting, I met a counselor who invited me to join a women's therapy group that met once a week. Although this group was not affiliated with AA, I received a great deal of help and support in dealing with my problems.

Teaching part-time at the community college level allowed more flexibility in my schedule and I could be home more for Andy and Mike and pursue my own interests. I began playing racquetball before my breast surgery and continued to play as soon as possible following the surgery. My other activities included jogging and walking whenever possible. The physical activity was an effective stress reducer for me.

Andy was still not doing well in eighth grade, but he was having fun. 'Fun loving Andy' his friends called him. However, I do not think any of his friends thought he was very bright. He was now the 'class clown', driving the teachers crazy and doing as little school work as possible. He had a wonderful laugh from deep down inside and he found that his laugh delighted people. He liked to laugh and he wanted people to like him. Although one teacher took a dislike to his disruptive behavior and gave him a detention for laughing while on a bus during a field trip. Even the other mothers told me that the punishment by the teacher was unfair. I was not teaching at St. Francis then and Andy did not want me to interfere, so I did not. I will never forget what this teacher did to my son, although she was a novice and did not know how to supervise and discipline adolescents.

Nevertheless, I cannot condone what she did, or those teachers like her who try to destroy the spirit of our children. My understanding is she has changed since this incident and is now an exceptional teacher. I hope this is true for the sake of the children she is now responsible for teaching.

When Andy was twelve, we decided to take a foreign exchange student into our home.

The principal at St. Francis told me about the foreign ex–change program. My thought was that having a student from another country living with us would be fun. I also hoped having a foreign exchange student would benefit Andy by exposing him to another culture. We contacted an organiza-tion to discuss participation in the exchange program. My con-tact in the program was unbelievably incompetent, and I would have been horrified if she had been handling the place-ment of my child in a foreign home. We never met her, com-municating only by telephone. No one from the organization ever came to my house to examine our lifestyle. We could have been any kind of pervert and no one would have known.

Within a month of the contact with her we agreed to have a fourteen-year-old boy from France come to live with us for a year; he would arrive in August. We were surprised one night to receive a call from Jean Charles Meunier, our exchange stu-dent. He was at the Phoenix airport. I was stunned to think of this young boy arriving in a foreign country by himself with no one to meet him. The contact person had given us the wrong date, and Jean Charles had missed his connecting flight in New York. Imagine a naive fourteen-year-old boy on his own at Kennedy Airport? Anyway, Mike, Andy and I rushed to the airport in Phoenix to pick him up. There stood a little boy who looked like Beaver on 'Leave It to Beaver', with big dark eyes and his hair standing straight up on his head. We had been assured he spoke English, but his English was not fluent. My French from my high school days was even worse.

In 1986 Andy entered the eighth grade and Jean Charles started as a freshman at Central High School. Jean Charles was a very pleasant young boy. He fit easily into our family. He and

Andy got along well, but never established a really close brotherly relationship. Jean Charles was much more mature than Andy and they had very different interests. Jean Charles liked music and sightseeing. He loved Mexican food and could not wait to see a real Indian. Jean Charles took three classes in ESL (English as a second language) at Central, and by Christmas was speaking excellent English. He has since returned to France and graduated from college in linguistics. He recently informed us that he is starting to teach English at a high school in his own country.

In France, a teacher starts teaching one class only and progressively moves into teaching more classes as they become more proficient. This system makes more sense to me than the way we throw first-year teachers into the classroom with no supervisory support.

I remember that we did more activities as a family while Jean Charles was living with us, so that he could experience as much of Arizona as possible. Occasionally, the boys were required to do a few chores, but not many. I was again home more, so I did everything around the house myself.

Once we hiked with some friends down the south rim of the Grand Canyon to Havasu Falls. There were about twenty-six people in our group, with many children. Andy's cousins, Shawn and David, hiked down with their mother Julie, so Andy had someone he knew to accompany him. Hiking was not Andy's choice of hobbies. He was okay going down to the Falls, because he was with David and Shawn, but on the way out he was miserable. He lagged along and had to be coaxed most of the way back to trail head. Other friends of ours walked with him because they were walking a slower pace than the leaders. The trail is a ten-mile hike down and another ten out, and Andy should have handled the walk. His behavior embarrassed me, and I think Mike, too. Andy had plenty of energy to play games with his friends, but any activity that required walking or running was a struggle. I have often questioned the causes for his lack of stamina.

Another time, our family went on a camping trip with members of Mike's family over a holiday weekend. David and Shawn were again with us. As usual, one morning Andy slept while the family went on a walk to explore, although David and Shawn went hiking with the group. Andy was consistent in his attitude toward any physical exercise. He was putting on weight, but not eating healthy foods. He was very stubborn and I could never convince him to take vitamins or food supplements.

Andy completed eighth grade at St. Francis and graduated with average grades. His grades were definitely not high enough to be admitted to Brophy with his friend Richard. Richard had begun to move away from Andy, spending more time with other friends. Richard was a serious student, and his parents were determined that he would do well and succeed in school. They were always kind to Andy, but seemed to know Andy was not a serious student, and was not going in the same direction they wanted for their son. Richard choosing to be with other friends hurt Andy, although I do not think he really understood the dynamics of what was happening. I understood what was happening with Richard and the change hurt me too. Nevertheless, I rationalized how his parents felt. Richard was beginning to mature, and Andy was not. Andy never wanted to be an adult. He told me this himself some years later.

Mike and I were torn whether to send Andy to St. Mary's High School where Mike had graduated, or Brophy. Andy wanted to go to Brophy because all his friends from St. Francis were going there. We were not sure what was best for Andy, but wanted whatever Andy wanted. In all honesty, Brophy had such an outstanding academic reputation I really wanted Andy to be able to graduate from there. I thought the faculty could teach him and get him on track academically.

We gave Andy the choice of St. Mary's High School or Brophy College Preparatory. He chose Brophy. The only way the school would accept him was if he improved his grades in English and math. He had to go to summer school and get at least a 'B' in each course to be accepted. He and Richard both attended summer school and took English and math. Andy received an 'A' in math and a 'B' in English, showing that he could apply himself when he wanted. I think Richard was a little miffed because Andy did better than he in math, as Richard was generally much more competitive than Andy. This pattern of Andy doing well for a short period of time was the constant theme throughout his life; he seemed unable to remain focused on any task for extended periods. He would always start school in September doing well, but after the first nine weeks his attention span faded. My hope was that high school would be different.

> *"Risk Factors for Adolescent Suicidal Episodes:*
> *Poor impulse control, stressful life events,*
> *humiliating experiences and interpersonal*
> *relationships."*
>
> *'Adolescent Suicide Task Force 1994'*

ANDY, WHY DID YOU HAVE TO GO?

*"Every blade of grass has its Angel that bends
over it and whispers grow, grow."*

Talmud

[6]

Brophy College Preparatory

Brophy is an exceptional college preparatory school with a history of academic excellence since 1952. The school was traditionally an all-boys school; Xavier, directly behind Brophy, is an all-girls school, but in recent years a few classes in both schools have become coed. The Jesuit priests originally founded the high school in 1928 when Mrs. William H. Brophy donated the property and sufficient funds to build a Jesuit school in memory of her husband, who died in 1922. The Jesuit order is a teaching order that takes great pride in an academic history that dates back to St. Ignatius of Loyola, 1491-1556. The competition for admission is keen among outstanding junior high students from public and private schools throughout the Valley. Catholic children attending a parochial elementary school are usually given priority over non-Catholic students. Parents feel privileged to have their child attend Brophy, an honor the young men are expected to accept by doing well.

Mike attended St. Mary's High School when he was a teenager, and the rivalry between Brophy and St. Mary's is a tradition as old as the schools themselves. The Franciscan priests founded St Mary's in 1917; the Franciscans follow the classical teaching of St. Francis of Assisi. The school, in addition to academic emphasis, is also known for their traditionally successful football team. Mike would have preferred that Andy attend St. Mary's but would never have insisted. Mike has many friends who graduated from Brophy, and as adults, they maintain a friendly rivalry.

In 1989 Andy started Brophy very excited about entering high school. He thought he and Richard would continue to be close friends as they had been in elementary school. After a very short time into the school year Richard clearly indicated he was taking high school very seriously. He no longer had time to play as much with Andy. Andy did not understand this change in Richard's attitude. When he called Richard to come over, Richard was too busy doing homework or was going to Jason's house. Richard began to cultivate his friendship with Jason, another boy with whom he and Andy had gone to grammar school. Jason was a serious boy who was also an excellent student. Jason was the oldest of three sons whose mother was a fifth-grade teacher at St. Francis. Andy knew Jason, but had never formed a friendship, choosing to be with Richard whenever possible. Andy had many friends, but Richard was always his first choice for someone to invite over for the weekend. If Richard could not come over, then Andy would invite other friends.

Andy started Brophy applying himself academically, but after the first nine weeks reverted to his old pattern. He used one excuse after another to avoid doing his homework, and we fell into the same old pattern of my nagging and him procrastinating. Andy completed the first year of high school with average grades. His grades were unremarkable, but he passed all subjects with a C+ or better. Andy was taking a college preparatory curriculum of algebra, English, science, religion and creative writing. Initially, his father and I were encouraged with his grades, thinking he was finally taking school seriously. But, our optimism was short-lived.

Andy's friendship with Richard cooled greatly during their freshman year. Andy never told me what happened between them, but by the end of the school year, Richard was no longer a major part of his life. Richard said 'no' more than 'yes' to Andy's frequent invitations to come over. Other boys Andy had known at St. Francis now became his companions. Tim was one of those boys; he was in the same grade as Andy. His mother was a second-grade teacher at St. Francis. Tim was the youngest of two boys in his family and fun loving. His mother kept a close watch on him, making sure he did his work, and dealing with him firmly if he fell behind.

Another friend was Paul, a classmate who had come to St. Francis in the sixth grade after moving to Phoenix from Texas. Paul had an older sister and was the youngest child in his family. Again, Paul's mother kept a close watch on his academic performance, and homework limited his freedom. Andy had other friends from St. Francis if his favorite friends were unavailable. Andy's sense of humor was attractive to the parents as well as his classmates. Richard, Jason, Tim and Paul, in that order, were Andy's best friends from St. Francis school days.

As mentioned in the previous chapter, in 1984 while Andy was still in grammar school we began to take summer vacations as a family in Mission Beach. There on the beach, escaping the summer heat, many of our friends from Phoenix, including Andy's friends were enjoying the ocean.

One summer, Richard came with us to Mission Beach; this was the summer between the boys' seventh and eighth-grade years at St. Francis. Andy made friends with other youngsters visiting Mission Beach. I think an incident happened involving these other children, a boy and his sister, that Richard did not like because he suddenly wanted to go home early. Richard's mother and I had agreed that if he wanted to leave before us we would send him home by plane. We took him to the San Diego airport where we saw him board a plane to Phoenix. Mike and I never discovered why he went home.

Our house had always been a gathering place for Andy and his friends. Once, I recall, a Kool-aid commercial showed a mother serving Kool-aid to her son and the neighborhood kids. I jokingly called myself the 'Kool-aid mom'. I liked having the house full of boys and encouraged Andy to have his friends over whenever possible. By having the boys at our home we could keep an eye on their activities. I knew Andy was safe when he was at the homes of other families, but he preferred having his friends come to our home as much as possible. Our backyard has sixteen orange trees, bushes, and lawn for games. We added a play pool when Andy was nine or ten years old. The boys spent many happy hours playing hide and seek, G. I. Joe, and whatever other games came to mind. The games became more complicated as the boys grew older. Andy had a creative imagination and could come up with new twists to old games. The game *Dungeons and Dragons* became popular about the time Andy was in junior high school and he and his buddies would role-play *Dungeons* for hours.

Andy was very friendly with the children next door. Their mother took care of him for a few years when I was working, and the children became friends. The daughter, Kathy, was about two years older than Andy; and there were two younger boys. Tommy was about four years younger than Andy and the youngest boy, Michael, was six years younger. Andy and these children were very close and behaved as if they were sister and brothers. When Andy did not have his friends from school for company, he had Tommy and Michael. Being older than the two brothers, he could boss them around and be in charge, but he was never mean to them. The parents of these children divorced, and after a year or so, the family moved away. Andy lost touch with them until several years later when the children and their mother moved back into our neighborhood. The three boys getting together would become a sporadic occurrence; long periods passed when Andy would not see or visit with them. Kathy and the boys would call when they needed help from Andy.

He began the role of rescuer early in his high school years. Kathy was having difficulty in her teenage years and could always rely on 'big brother' Andy to take care of her. He treated her like a little sister, because she was much smaller physically. Kathy had an abusive boy friend who would knock her around. When she came to Andy, he would protect her, and tell the boy friend to get lost. The boy friend apparently had only enough courage to hit women. Andy grew to be six feet tall, and Kathy's boy friend was always pleasant when Andy was around. The brothers, Tommy and Michael, would also rely on Andy if they needed a big brother. Andy loved the role of big brother riding to the rescue. He was always helping others, even to his own detriment.

I must confess he learned this behavior from me. Throughout Andy's entire life I was always rescuing someone. In San Francisco, I cared for three children, a little girl Andy's age, and her two older brothers. Their mother was in a mental institution, and the father was struggling to keep his family together. These children were so pathetic, and already so damaged, that I provided care for them until the problems became too many for me to manage.

Years later, in Phoenix, after our foreign exchange student returned to France, one of my nephews came to stay with us. He was a heroin addict. Soon, thereafter, another nephew came to stay, and he was also a heroin addict. The boys were cousins. I could not handle two addicts, so I asked the nephew who arrived first to leave. The first nephew, Mark, had already been with us more than six months, and he was actively using heroin and lying to us. Initially, the reason Mark came to live with us was because he wanted to stop using drugs and needed to get away from his environment. We believed him, but we made the rules clear that if he started using again, he would have to leave.

Now Michael, the other nephew was in serious trouble and claimed he was trying to quit heroin. I felt I had to help him. Mike always went along with my rescue missions, although the decision to support all the people I kept dragging home cost him financially. Michael stayed with us almost a year. After he started working at a job Mike had arranged for him he started using heroin again. After all of Mark's lies about not using, we did not give Michael a second chance. I told him to leave, and after taking him to pick up his paycheck, took him to the bus depot. In thanks for our support and help, he later robbed us while we were vacationing in Mexico.

Mike, Andy, and I had gone to Rocky Point, Mexico, to stay for a weekend with friends who owned a house at the beach. These friends had two daughters and Andy knew the family from other times when we had been together. The girls were four years apart in age, and Andy was in the middle. Andy had a great time riding a three-wheeler on the beach and we could see him racing back and forth down the beach. He left the three-wheeler only long enough to eat and sleep. The oldest girl's boy friend also came along on the trip and they spent time together. The youngest daughter, a few years younger than Andy, hung out with her father most of the time.

In the meantime Mike and I were very concerned about Michael being in Phoenix. We had a strong feeling that Michael was going to retaliate against us in some way while we were out of town. Sure enough, when we returned home Mike's car was gone, and so were the television sets and miscellaneous items. We called the police and an officer came to the house and made a report. The police recovered our car in South Phoenix a few days later. The car was full of drug paraphernalia, used needles and syringes.

A few weeks later the police found Michael and arrested him. The arrest was the best thing that ever happened to him. I went to see Michael in jail, and continued to visit him on a regular basis. Michael was very ashamed of what he had done to the two people he loved. With Mike's approval, we gave him some financial support the entire two years he was in prison. Michael was truly sorry for what he had done, and has remained clean and sober for more than ten years. He is now a drug rehabilitation counselor in Southern California.

Perhaps I should explain my involvement with my nephews. My two sisters are many years older than I am. My nephew, Michael, was born to my oldest sister when I was ten years old. Michael's mother was not happy about his birth because she was not married at the time. I became attached to Michael by baby-sitting him whenever possible. Michael was the firstborn of five children. My role was being a second mom to him, the mom on whom he could always count. My other sister's oldest son is Mark. He was the first nephew to come to stay with us. Although I had never spent time with him when he was young, I loved him dearly. He deeply saddened me when he, too, became addicted to heroin like his cousin Michael. In my egotism I thought I could help Mark overcome his addiction. Unfortunately, I could not. Another ten years would pass before Mark would reach his bottom. Today, thank God, he is finally clean and sober. Both young men had been heroin users for more than twenty years before they were free of drugs and changed their lives to become responsible and self-sufficient people.

Where was Andy during my saving of mankind? Andy was right there, observing my rescue attempts, and being the same happy child as always. I probably neglected him in all this rescuing. Certainly, I neglected my husband; however, neither Mike nor Andy ever complained. Perhaps because they enjoyed the cousins. Michael and Mark were both adults, and did things with Andy as a big brother might. Michael took Andy to race slot cars, and Mark would take time to play ball with him.

Mark and Michael lived with us for a year and a half, during Andy's eighth and ninth-grade years in school. After they left, Mike's brother Bill came to live with us. Bill has rheumatoid arthritis of the spine. In addition, Bill is an alcoholic and had reached his bottom. He had no money, no home, and no other family members wanted to care for him. Mike and I agreed to allow Bill to live with us if he stopped drinking. He accepted our conditions and came to live with us. Shortly after Bill moved in with us, his girl friend was murdered in Phoenix by her estranged husband who committed suicide immediately after killing her. The murder devastated Bill, who started drinking again, but he tried to hide the fact. After six months or more Mike and I decided we could not ignore Bill's drinking. We contacted a halfway house for alcoholics and made arrangements for him to move there. Bill lived in the halfway house for about seven months, after which Mike helped him find a job with a construction firm as a truck driver.

Andy was aware of these events and was very supportive of our efforts. Andy even joined a family intervention planned for Bill, but which never happened because Bill voluntarily entered a rehabilitation program.

As previously mentioned, during the eighth and ninth grade Andy began to gain weight. Andy liked McDonald's Happy Meals, and I often bought those for him. He continued eating fast food and gaining weight. He went out for the football team but did not make the 'cut'. Andy was a 'late bloomer', one of those children who go through puberty later than most. He was fifteen before he started developing body hair, and the accompanying physical changes of puberty. As Andy gained weight he became more sedentary, playing *Nintendo*, and games that did not require physical activity. He retained his chubby look until his junior year in high school.

Andy's birth date is July 19, 1973. He turned sixteen during the summer between his freshman and sophomore years in high school. Andy always had a fascination with cars. He had every *Hot Wheels* car ever made, and I think he was making 'varoom' sounds while still in the womb. By the time he was two years old he was motoring all over the house with his cars, going 'varoom, varoom'. Andy could hardly wait to drive, and during the summer of 1989 he learned to drive. His father and I taught him, and he also attended drivers' education at the local high school.

In his sophomore year at Brophy, Andy was one of the few boys allowed to drive, and access to a car made him popular. Andy's self-esteem seemed very low to me at this time. His best friend had seemingly abandoned him, and he was just beginning to experience puberty. Andy was really struggling with the idea of growing up and not knowing what to do about the changes in his life. Sometimes he would come home and play with his *G.I. Joe* figures in his room, pretending he was a child again. To see him going through the pangs of adolescence was very sad for me. Andy became less willing to express to me what he was feeling. Because I was supportive and not wishing to invade his privacy, I could only wait for him to approach me with a question or to talk.

Mike never found time to discuss with Andy the changes that go on within an adolescent male. Perhaps, Mike did not know what to say to Andy. Mike's father had never discussed sex and male changes with him and he had no clue how to talk to Andy. Now, Andy was struggling emotionally as well as academically; having never been an adolescent male, there was no way for me to help him. Andy needed male guidance, and I could not give him the understanding he needed to resolve his issues.

Mike and I fought about Andy often during these years. Mike had started working at age twelve and he matured much earlier than Andy. He could not relate to the physical and hormonal changes his son was experiencing. By the time Mike was sixteen he was working full-time, and helping his family financially. Mike thought all Andy needed was some space to grow up and he would be all right. After all, Mike's father never told him anything about sex, or was involved in his teenage years, and look how well Mike turned out. I argued, futilely, that Andy was different and needed his father's guidance. The 'bonding' relationship between father and son never happened.

I felt that if Andy had a driver's license the privilege would help his self-esteem. Of course, he did not have his own car and drove his father's Ford Fairmont occasionally. My Buick was a newer car and we did not want Andy driving our best vehicle. We allowed Andy to drive the Ford on the weekends when his father was not using the car. One night about eleven o'clock we received a call from Andy. He had been in an automobile accident. His cousin David was with him. They were all right, but the car was not. The story was that Andy swerved in the rain to miss a cat and the car spun out on the slick street, striking the curb. The rear axle on the car was broken. Mike and I had just a few months earlier reduced the insurance on the Ford to liability only. This meant there was no coverage for the physical damage to the car. The damage was $2,500, more than the car was worth. We decided not to have the car repaired, and sold the wreck for salvage. Mike then leased a new 1989 Chevrolet Silverado pickup truck. The truck was a beauty, and we told Andy 'hands off'.

This left my Buick for Andy to borrow on occasion. As mentioned in an earlier chapter, I found saying 'no' to Andy or anyone I care about almost impossible. Surprise, surprise, within a few months, Andy was in a wreck with my car, this time, after school and on his way to our home with a friend. The accident occurred at an intersection. Andy was in the middle of the intersection behind a car that was turning left; when this car turned left, the signal light turned red. Andy finished going through the intersection and was struck broadside by a car coming from the other direction. Again, fortunately, no one was hurt. Andy and his friend walked home from the accident; they were only a few miles from home.

The police did not give Andy a citation, but our insurance company decided he was partially at fault. The insurance company settled the claim with the other insurance carrier by simply splitting the damages. This decision appalled me because now Andy would have an accident charged against him although he was not at fault in the incident. The insurance rate for male teenage drivers is costly enough, but with an accident charged against the teenager, the insurance premium is outrageous.

The Buick was struck between the front and rear passengers' door, bending the frame. The damage was as much as the car was worth, and the adjuster told us once the frame is bent, the car will never drive the same. Again, we decided not to have the car repaired. We took the money and bought an older model Oldsmobile. When I say old, I mean 1970 vintage. Our mechanic owned the Oldsmobile and offered to sell us the car. We trusted our mechanic and felt the Olds would be a good buy. The car was mechanically sound with a 350-hp engine, that registered about twelve miles to the gallon of gas. Andy and his friends lovingly called the car the 'booger' because the car was green. I called the car a tank because the Olds was so big and heavy. At least, Andy was safe when he was driving the 'booger'. The 'booger' was definitely not cool for a sixteen year-old to drive.

Hindsight tells me that we probably should have pulled Andy's driver's license and let him mature. He really was not driving recklessly that we could tell, so the accidents did not seem to call for the removal of his license. On the way to church one morning we saw a Ford Mustang for sale. I thought if Andy had his own car he would be more careful and take pride in ownership. The car was a white 1977 model, with a 350-hp engine. The car needed work, but the price was right. Andy loved the car on sight so we bought the Mustang.

Two months after spending more than $3,000 repairing the car, an elderly driver hit the car, which was totaled. The police cited the other driver, but his insurance company did not want to make a fair settlement. I telephoned a family friend, an attorney, and asked him to contact the other driver's insurance company for us. He was kind enough to do this and we received total reimbursement for our loss. Nothing was ever easy where Andy was involved. These accidents happened within six months of Andy receiving his driver's license, and he was not legally at fault in any of them. Fortunately, no one was hurt in the accidents.

As I write about this period, I am amazed at what went on then, and how poorly we handled the decisions which involved Andy: we were too closely and emotionally involved to see the obvious. Mike was firmly convinced that Andy was simply going through an adolescent phase. Mike always believed Andy would mature without incident. He was sure by being faithful to God, that God in turn would keep Andy safe. On the other hand I was terrified, and experienced horrible premonitions that my beloved son was going to die young.

When Andy was sixteen I shared these thoughts with a friend. She was struggling over problems with her son, who was older than Andy, and assured me that Andy's behavior was normal. Did my worry make his death happen? Some readers may say these premonitions were a 'self-fulfilling prophecy'. I have often wondered if I did make his death happen. In truth, Mike and I always encouraged Andy, reassuring him he could accomplish whatever he desired. I believed in him, but maybe his sensitive soul picked up on my fear and influenced his behavior.

As Andy did very poorly at Brophy his sophomore year, the dean of students put him on academic probation. Andy's guidance counselor felt that Andy really did not belong at Brophy. I felt the counselor had done nothing to encourage or help Andy, and finally persuaded another teacher to be Andy's counselor. This counselor had a delightful sense of humor and seemed to take a genuine interest in the boys. I was again mistaken. His interest in Andy was limited to asking him about his school work. Andy would flash that fabulous smile and say 'fine' and that would be the end of the counseling session. Andy was definitely not applying himself at school. He was too busy chauffeuring his friends around town. I always felt that the friends took advantage of his good nature, but to Andy his friends and driving the car meant everything to him. He did not care about anything else. I nagged, pleaded, talked and yelled at Andy. Nothing I said or did made an impression on him.

Eventually, Andy started having problems sleeping at night, although sleeping had never been a problem in the past. The sleeplessness seemed to coincide with the onset of puberty; Andy became very nervous and irritable. In teaching psychology classes I would sometimes jokingly say that I suspected a 'changeling' had come and switched places with my son. A changeling is a fictional character who supposedly switches places with a real person. The change in Andy's personality was dramatic. He was a completely different person than he had been before adolescence.

Andy would not listen to me and began to be very disrespectful. His attitude made Mike furious and sometimes he would yell at Andy. Their relationship continued to deteriorate, and I was the buffer between the two of them. Mike would tell me what Andy was doing wrong, and I was to tell Andy to correct his attitude. Andy would tell me how his father mistreated him, and I was to tell Mike. I was always in the middle and did not have enough experience to step back and make them deal with each other directly. Now that the situation is ended, I can see clearly what was happening at the time. In the moment, though, the emotional involvement is too strong to see the situation clearly. We were in a vicious cycle and none of us knew how to stop the process.

Mike and I had quit drinking alcohol. We did not want to

be hypocrites, telling Andy not to get involved with alcohol, while we continued to drink. I was still going to AA meetings and working on staying sober. Both Mike and I have alcoholism in our families, and we were afraid Andy would develop a drinking problem. We hoped by modeling behavior not involving alcohol Andy would follow our example. I talked honestly with Andy about alcoholism in the family and my battle with alcohol. I spoke with him about illegal drugs, smoking and the responsibility of being sexually active too young. I was adamant about the responsibility involved in bringing an innocent child into the world. We told him that he would be financially responsible for any child he fathered. Andy listened politely, and assured us he would not do any of the things we were cautioning him about.

In retrospect, Andy seemed to reject everything we valued and believed. He started smoking after I cautioned him that smoking was addictive. I have never smoked, except to try cigarettes when I was a teenager, and Mike quit smoking the first year Andy was born. Andy assured me he was just smoking occasionally, but smoking soon became a habit. He never smoked in the house and was always considerate about not smoking around me.

We furnished the 'Arizona room' in our house as a place for Andy and his friends; a television, couch and stereo. The young people tended to congregate at our house. This was a good plan because I could keep an eye on them. Unfortunately, the boys began to sneak beer into the Arizona room. If I caught them, I would lecture Andy about drinking, and he would promise he would not have beer in the house anymore. How could these teenagers buy beer? I found out Andy had a fake identification, showing his age as twenty-one. I confiscated the identification and gave him another lecture. I was naive;

buying alcohol and drugs is never a problem for teenagers, and buying beer was no problem for Andy and his friends. Drinking is very popular among the teenage population and Andy's group was no different.

One summer when Andy was seventeen we rented a large apartment in Mission Beach for two weeks and allowed Andy to bring one of his friends. Several of Andy's other friends were also going to be in Mission Beach at the same time. The end result was we usually had four boys staying at our place, rather than two. During this vacation Mike and I had to fly home to Phoenix for a weekend and were concerned about leaving teenagers at the apartment unsupervised. They of course assured us they would be fine, and there would be no wild parties. We asked Mike's friends, Bob and Mary, who were renting a house a few blocks away to check on the boys on Saturday night.

When we returned, Bob and Mary had quite a story to tell. Bob went to the apartment on Saturday night, and found the apartment full of young people, wall to wall, and hanging off the balcony. He was furious, and told Andy to ask them to leave and to clean up the place. Andy and Tim chased everyone out of the apartment and did all the clean up, so that when Bob returned an hour later the apartment was back to normal. Bob could hardly keep a straight face when telling us the tale. He said he had never seen so many young people in one place in his entire life, and that Andy really knew how to throw a party. Bob and Mike in their youth had thrown a few wild parties themselves.

We confronted Andy about the party. He claimed he had not invited all those young people, one of the other boys had, and he had been unable to stop the party from happening. I doubt this is true, but we have never heard the true story. Andy may have been telling the truth.

The next school year, Andy's junior year, his grades did not improve. How could they, if he stopped even trying to do his homework? His friends were all-important. He was waking early every morning and picking up a friend to take to Brophy, then he would fall asleep in class. His friends called our home all hours of the day and night. Andy had a telephone in his room and was always on the phone; I worried about the calls but Mike assured me Andy was just being a normal teenager, and 'would grow up and be fine'.

We asked Andy if he wanted to drop out of Brophy and go to St. Mary's, and he said 'no' he wanted to attend Brophy. I wish now we had sent him to St. Mary's his junior year, but hindsight is always twenty-twenty. During Andy's junior year he fell in love with a girl who attended Xavier High School. This encounter would prove traumatic for both youngsters.

In 1991, Andy's junior year, I had accepted a one-year contract to teach a computer-based program through Glendale Community College. My hours were 11:00 a.m. to 7:00 p.m. five days a week. These hours meant that neither parent was home when Andy returned from school. Andy began to ditch classes with his girl friend and both would come to our house. Mike came home one day and found them in a compromising situation. Mike was furious, and Andy and the girl were embarrassed. Mike called me at work and told me what happened. After arriving home I talked with Andy. He assured me nothing had happened sexually, and he would not bring a girl to our house while Mike and I were gone.

A few months later, Andy and the girl broke up; rather she broke up with him. Andy was devastated. He tried to win her back. Many nights I could hear him crying by the pool. His heart rending sobs tore my heart. I did not want to invade his privacy and so I let him cry. Andy lost more than ten pounds during the breakup. Unfortunately, the two of them soon got back together. Their 'yo-yo' relationship was to continue for several years. By the time Andy was nineteen years old, our doctor diagnosed him with an ulcer, probably related to this devastating relationship. Andy even jokingly named his ulcer after the girl.

Following the latest automobile accident, we replaced the wrecked Mustang with a red Pontiac Firebird. One evening Andy came home and told us he had received a hit-and-run citation. Andy had received a phone call from this girl friend, and he was so upset about the call that he jumped into his car and raced to her house. While speeding to her house he missed a corner and ran into a wooden fence. The fence was slightly damaged and there was no damage to Andy's car. Instead of staying at the scene of the accident, he left and drove to his girl friend's house. The accident happened three blocks from our house and neighbors had identified his car for the police. A police car cruised the neighborhood and when Andy returned home the police stopped him. He readily admitted the accident and the officer cited him for speeding and leaving the scene. Naturally, his father and I were shocked and disappointed. We grounded Andy.

We hired an attorney to represent Andy in court, because this was a serious offense, and we had no idea what penalty the court would impose. The attorney was not cheap and we were not really sure how much he helped the case. The attorney had Andy plead guilty and Andy was fined and his license suspended for three months. Mike and I went to court with him and were surprised to see the prosecutor with about five people as witnesses in the case. I guess the people had seen the accident, and since Andy had been speeding in their neighborhood in the past they wanted to punish him. Because Andy pleaded guilty the attorneys did not call the witnesses. The damage to the fence was minimal. One post had to be replaced, and I think the cost was $100. There was no damage to Andy's car. The real problem was Andy leaving the scene of the accident.

Mike and I have always been responsible people, even when we were young, and we could not understand Andy's behavior. To me, this was the straw that broke the camel's back. I forced Andy to go with me to see a psychologist friend of mine who did a complete psychological evaluation on him. He was very angry with me for making him talk to the psychologist, but submitted to the testing and evaluation, grudgingly.

The tests, a complete battery of psychological and cognitive testing, and results were completed and evaluated in one day. Andy's I. Q. was in the high range of average, with exceptional verbal abilities. His scores on a dictation test for English and history placed him much lower than his peers. Based on Federal Guidelines and the State of Arizona criterion for specific learning disability, he exhibited a discrepancy between his cognitive potential and his achievement. Therefore, the public education guidelines could qualify him as 'learning disabled'. The tests did not reveal whether his learning problem was a specific developmental disorder (i.e., language) or poor motivation or another functional process. On the *Bender Visual-Motor Gestalt,* his drawings suggested some mild visual-motor difficulties and disorganization.

The *Bender Visual-Motor Gestalt Test* is one of the most widely used neuropyschological tests, consisting of nine cards, each displaying a simple design. Bender Gestalt Test subjects look at the designs one at a time and copy each one on a piece of paper. Later they try to redraw the designs from memory.

By the age of twelve, most people can remember and redraw the designs accurately. Notable errors in accuracy are thought to reflect organic brain impairment.

Andy's personality profile revealed he was having an unusually large number of personal and emotional problems. He was found to have a great deal of overt anxiety, and indications of problematic depression. Psychologists describe individuals with profiles similar to Andy's as impulsive, energetic people who, lacking professional intervention, may become psychologically maladjusted.

Regarding the diagnosis of a learning disability, the psychologist found no indicators of physiological and/or biological causes. There were several indicators of functional deficits. Andy's *Kinetic Family Drawing* revealed a general level of immaturity and some emotional indicators. His performances on the *Bender* test suggested mild visual-motor difficulty. His profile revealed an angry young man with an antagonistic attitude toward any psychological treatment. The psychologist recommended further evaluation to rule out more chronic distress. He also recommended counseling to focus on the nature of his distress, and possible solutions. Family counseling was also recommended. The psychologist felt that because of the hostile way Andy was forced into evaluation he could not work with Andy and suggested another therapist.

Armed with this report, I spoke with Andy and his father. Andy refused to be evaluated for a 'learning disability', or consider any remedial help from school. Brophy did not offer this type of assistance, but the public school system did have a program. After many discussions Andy did agree to go to counseling with us. We found a male therapist, and the three of us saw him once a week for a month or two. Andy felt we, his parents, were uniting against him in the sessions. Mike and I agreed to stop coming to the sessions with Andy if he would continue seeing the therapist at least once a week. Andy agreed to this arrangement and went faithfully for about three months. Andy appeared to be responding to his sessions. The therapist, pleading confidentiality, did not offer to share information Andy discussed with him. The only thing I remember him telling me was that Andy would just have to 'hit the wall', before he would change. I took this statement to mean Andy was going to have to learn his lessons the hard way, as usual.

After three months Andy asked to stop attending the sessions; and the counselor agreed. Mike and I continued to see the therapist for marriage counseling. This therapist is the counselor I mentioned earlier who sang *Cat's in a Cradle* to Mike during one of our sessions. The song caused me to cry, and caused Mike to look confused.

In the meantime, the motor vehicle department returned Andy's license three months after the suspension. Andy's behavior toward us and his attitude in school was much improved. I spoke with friends about Andy and they simply felt Mike and I should practice 'tough love' and let Andy suffer the consequences of his actions; easy for them to say. These well-meaning people did not know Andy, or what frustrations he was experiencing.

In the summer of 1991 we received a letter from Brophy advising us that Andy had not improved his grades, and that he was suspended from school. While Andy was in therapy, I had gone to the president of Brophy and told him Andy's situation. He was very understanding. He told me about his own brother, who had struggled through adolescence before getting his life on track. Everywhere I turned, parents and teachers told me Andy was just having a rough time going through adolescence: that he was basically a good kid, with good parents, and his life would 'turn out all right', we just needed to let him 'suffer the consequences of his actions'.

> *'One failure after another. One loss after another, adds up to low self-esteem. Being diagnosed at seventeen years of age with learning disorder is too late. Advice is cheap and easy when the child involved is not your own. Knowing the right thing to do is only easy for those not involved at the time. The experts do not have all the answers, they can only recommend.'*
>
> *'In retrospect:' JG*

The Lost Years

During Andy's junior year he met his first love, and this relationship probably influenced his lack of interest in school. I was still working a one-year contract through Glendale Community College that kept me away from home from noon to late evening. Mike was working his usual fifty to fifty-five hours a week, and Andy was left with little supervision.

In Andy's junior year at Brophy he was failing and the staff advised us that Andy would not be able to return the following school year. Mike and I gave him the choice of going to St. Mary's or public school. Andy said he did not care which school he attended. At this time we were getting advice from friends regarding Andy's behavior. These friends said we needed to let Andy suffer the consequences of his actions, that Andy was too spoiled, and did not appreciate his advantages.

I was totally at a loss what action to take. I did not recognize the young man, who looked like my son, but acted nothing like my son. Mike did not know what to do either. He just kept telling me that Andy would be okay, because we were faithful to God, Andy would eventually be all right. We felt we had given him a good moral foundation, and we loved him with all our heart. I always believed the love I had for Andy and expressed to him would make up for the deficiencies in our parenting skills. Andy needed more help than we were capable of giving. Mike was from the generation of fathers who felt their responsibility was to provide comfort and security for their family, and the mother's job was to raise the children. Mike's friends, who were fathers, were experiencing similar relationships with their sons, and while they were not close with their sons during the teen years, they became closer in later years.

Daily, Andy was told by me that I loved him, and his father often told him he loved him, too; although not as often in his teen years as when he was a child. In my youth a family I knew always told each other daily that they loved one another. The parents explained to me the reason: in case something happened to a family member those left behind would not have to live with the regret of never having told the person how much they were loved. This tradition made a lasting impression on me, since no one ever told me as a child how much they loved me. As a child, I decided that when I married and had a family I would be sure to tell each member daily that I loved them. Mike and I started the same practice when we were married and continued when Andy was born. I am especially thankful for this custom now, because the last time I saw Andy alive, I told him I loved him, and he said he loved me, too.

In 1991 Andy started his senior year at Central High. Central was a magnet school that focused on foreign studies. Andy was 'zoned' to go to North High, which was farther from home, but by applying to the magnet program he was accepted at Central. This program started when desegregation was an issue in Arizona to encourage integrated student enrollment at inner city schools. To accomplish ethnic diversity each high school offered specific core subjects for each academic major. Central focused on foreign studies. At that time, Phoenix Union High School District (PUHSD) was suffering from declining enrollment, as white families moved out of Metro Phoenix, and minorities were left behind. Discrimination charges were brought against the PUHSD by the Federal EEOC in the 1960s and the district was mandated to desegregate, thereby prohibiting white students leaving the district to attend other schools.

Only in the past two years has the Federal law changed, allowing students in the PUHSD to attend a school outside the school district. Until then a parent needed a court order to move their child out of the PUHSD. I do not think in the past thirty years that any parent was able to get the court order approved enabling their child to go to a school outside of the district. Interestingly, when I told other parents about the desegregation law, no one had heard of the mandate. I even called our state representative for the district, and he too was ignorant of the law.

We found out about the federal mandate when we tried to enroll Andy in Shadow Mountain High School, a school outside the PUHSD. Andy's cousin Michael was only six weeks younger than Andy, and he attended this school. They were both at the same grade level. Michael and Andy were as different as night and day, with Michael being a serious, conservative young man. I was hoping that Andy, being around Michael, might benefit from his cousin's positive influence. Unfortunately, due to the law forcing Andy to stay in the PUHSD he could not attend Shadow Mountain.

We wish now we had enrolled him at St. Mary's, but once again, hindsight is twenty-twenty. St. Mary's was a Catholic high school with about six hundred students, and managed by

Franciscan priests. Brophy had one thousand students and a less personal approach to teaching than the smaller St. Mary's. The St. Francis Elementary school Andy attended had about four hundred children enrolled from kindergarten through eighth grade. Possibly, Andy was lost in the crowd at Brophy.

Andy had another cousin, David, who was a couple of years younger and a year behind Andy in grade level. David was attending St. Mary's but was not applying himself. This was part of the reason I was not excited about Andy attending St. Mary's. David and his friends might not be a positive influence on Andy. As a matter of fact, Andy's first encounter with the police occurred when he was with David and his friends. The incident with the police occurred while Andy was still sixteen and in his freshman year of high school.

One early evening I answered a knock on the door of our home and saw a policeman standing there. As soon as I saw the officer my thought was Andy had been in an accident and injured. The fear of Andy being in a car accident was a constant dread for me. Andy liked to drive fast and was not an experienced driver. He had already totaled his father's Ford Fairlane a few months after he started driving. The policeman asked if we owned a white Buick LeSabre. I answered yes, and explained that Andy had borrowed the car to meet David and his friends and was due to return by eight o'clock. The officer said the boys had stolen a twenty-pound bag of rice from an oriental food store. I was appalled.

As the officer was talking to me, Andy came home. I met Andy coming in through the kitchen, our usual way of entering the house. I told him the police were here, and asked if he and his friends had stolen the rice. Andy readily admitted the theft. The officer was very courteous, and probably saw the act as a boyish prank. However, as the officer spoke with him, Andy was very surly and uncooperative in naming his companions. I expressed surprise to Andy because of his attitude. He had never acted like a tough guy before. The officer and I were very angry at Andy's demeanor. The officer threatened to take him to jail, and I told Andy to stop acting like a hoodlum by being rude and belligerent. Andy then changed his attitude and tone of voice to a more respectful one, but was still reluctant to admit who had been involved with him. He did not want to 'rat' on his friends. The officer asked where the rice was located and what the boys planned to do with the contraband. Andy told us the bag was at the home of one of his friends, and the boys were planning to give the rice to the poor. The officer and I could not help grinning at this comment. Andy was told to retrieve the rice from his friend's house and return the rice to the store. Fortunately, no charges were pressed by the store owners.

The next day, I drove Andy to the grocery store and made him apologize to the owner while standing by his side. The owner was very polite and to my knowledge there was never another episode of Andy stealing.

David and his friends were with Andy when the rice was stolen. The negative incident with the rice, and the fact David had been with Andy when Andy had his first wreck in the Ford Fairlane, made me concerned that the boys would continue to cause mischief. My fear was that they would cause more trouble if they attended the same high school. What I did not know was that David's girl friend attended Central, so Andy would be around David anyway.

To be on track for graduation from high school, Andy needed to take United States History in summer school. Summer school was four mornings a week for two hours a day for five weeks. I forced Andy to attend, getting him up every morning, and making him attend school. Andy never did any homework, but achieved 'As' on his tests. I know, because I saw his test papers. On his final comprehensive exam covering the class material he received a score of 98 percent, but his grade for the course was a 'D' because he had not turned in homework. I called the school administrator and challenged the reasoning. I questioned what the teacher was trying to accomplish, teaching the subject matter, or the discipline of homework. The focus on homework rather than the comprehension of the course concepts is a serious flaw in the public education system in my opinion. The administrator agreed with my argument and offered to give Andy an oral exam. Andy could not be bothered to take the test. A grade of 'D' is passing, and he was not about to spend any more time in school.

Andy always had a wonderful memory. His ability to hear information, indicating that he was paying attention, remember the information and pass a test with an almost perfect score without reading the book or doing the homework was amazing. Not one teacher ever recognized or commended Andy on this exceptional ability. Instead, the teachers always reduced his final grade because he failed to turn in homework.

An acquaintance of mine was a secretary at Central High and met Andy after he started attending the school. She told me Andy was always pleasant, and never unruly or rude to her or his teachers. The truth is, Andy never applied himself at any school. If being kicked out of Brophy bothered him he never said anything to me about the fact. He claimed the students were all snobs at Brophy and he could not relate to them. He hung out with his friends when he was at school, being everyone's chauffeur. His cousin David's girl friend Andrea, who also attended Central, would hang out with Andy. She told me, after Andy died, that he was always there for the underdog. If anyone 'bullied' another student, Andy was there to stick up for the person, and make the other guy back down. By now, Andy was almost six feet tall, weighed 180 pounds and was not afraid to fight. Occasionally, Andy would come home with a shiner, but when asked how he managed to get the black eye, he would just grin and tell me the other guy looked worse. Andy was learning to be a 'tough guy'.

By Christmas of Andy's senior year at Central the situation was clear; he was not applying himself. He received another speeding ticket and his driver's license was again suspended for three months, even though he had gone to drivers' safety class for the first ticket he received. The record of his first speeding ticket had been removed from his motor vehicle license file, but the judge was tough and wanted to teach Andy a lesson. A three-month suspension of his driver's license was like a jail sentence to Andy. He would go outside to the driveway and sit in his Pontiac Firebird and smoke cigarettes.

The telephone never stopped ringing, with his friends calling him and wanting him to drive them some place. Several of his friends came by while his license was suspended and he would go out with them, but unlike Andy most of them did not have access to a car. To make sure he did not drive his car keys were taken away from him. He finally asked his dad if he could keep the keys in his pocket if he promised not to drive the car. Mike said 'okay', and gave Andy the keys. I suspect Andy was sneaking out with the car after we went to bed at night, but he made his way through the suspension without further incident, and his license was returned by the court. He was a very happy young man and, we hoped, a wiser one.

When we received Andy's first-semester report card from Central, he was flunking some of his classes and probably would not graduate from high school. The problem was, he was never in class, and never studied or did his homework. I talked with the school counselor and asked her to come to our home to help us talk with Andy. He was furious with me for suggesting that the counselor come to talk with us. Mike, the counselor and I tried to talk with him about school and how important graduating from high school and going to college would be to him and his future. The counselor was convinced Andy was doing drugs, and the drugs were the cause of his continued failure in high school. Andy swore that he was not doing any drugs other than alcohol. Andy was very resentful that the school counselor suggested that he was using drugs.

I have to confess that I, too, was afraid Andy was involved with drugs. Drugs were the only cause that seemed to make sense in the dramatic change in his behavior. Wanting to be informed I read books on symptoms of adolescent drug use. I always cleaned Andy's room, and while in his room looked for any sign of drugs or paraphernalia. I never found anything but beer bottle caps and cigarettes. Obviously, Andy and his friends were getting alcohol, even though they were underage. I knew some of Andy's friends were using drugs because Andy told me, but I could find no evidence of Andy using drugs. My suspicions were that he experimented with drugs early in adolescence, but decided against them, preferring alcohol. His friend Tim told me recently that he is sure Andy did not do drugs because Andy liked to be in control. He agreed Andy probably tried drugs, but said Andy was very vocal about the dangers of using drugs.

Andy was now nineteen and probably not going to graduate from high school. Mike and I told him if he was not going to graduate he might as well quit school and get a job. We were hoping the reality of working in a low-paying job would help him realize how important an education was, and would be encouraged to return to school once he found out that working for minimum wages was a dead end.

We had encouraged Andy when he was sixteen to find a summer job. That summer he did work as a clerk in an attorney's office for about five weeks, but then he was laid off because there was no work for him. After that job he always managed to stall around every summer and never find a summer job. At nineteen, a high school dropout, he began work as a security guard. He worked the night shift, and had the exciting job of guarding a sand and gravel pit. I would wake him about 11:00 p.m., fix his lunch, and get him off to work for the midnight shift. At first he was excited about being a security guard and wearing a uniform, but the thrill quickly wore off and within a few months he quit work.

Working interfered with Andy's social life. There were young people at our house every evening, many of them strangers to me. Andy's old friends from Brophy seldom came around during this period. The people he brought home were definitely not like the kids Andy had grown up with, or that met with our approval. Some of them were into drugs, and some of the girls used language that would make a sailor blush. The girls swore more than the boys and were less respectful toward me. The young people would congregate in the Arizona room after Mike and I went to bed at night. Occasionally, when the laughter and talking became too loud, I would get up and tell them to be quiet. I never wanted to embarrass Andy in front of his friends, so I would call him out of the room and ask him to quiet down the guests.

During this time a young man, Greg, who Andy probably met at a party started staying at our house. He would sleep on the floor in Andy's room. After a week or so I asked Andy what was going on and he told me the boy had been kicked out of his house by his father and needed a place to stay. We were not pleased with having a strange boy stay in our home uninvited, but did not have the heart to make him leave. He was quiet and polite, and never bothered anything or anyone. He just needed a place to sleep. Eventually, he ended up spending the better part of the summer with us, until college started. His grandmother was going to pay his tuition for college in the Fall, and he was going to live with her and attend school. Since Andy's death, he is one of the boys who continues to come by occasionally to say hello and see how we are doing. Greg fathered a son, who was born ten months after Andy's death. In memory of Andy, the new father gave his son the middle name of Andrew. Greg is now a devoted single father, struggling to be a responsible and loving parent.

Finding transient young people sleeping in Andy's room or in the Arizona room became a pattern. The young people were never a problem and we could not find the heart to make them leave. They were all so pathetic looking, and appeared so lost and forlorn that we felt sorry for them. The boys never caused any trouble for us, and in all the time we had kids wandering through our home, nothing was ever damaged or stolen. My guess is the kids knew their boundaries with Andy, and while he might let them stay in our house, he would not tolerate destruction of property or stealing. We appreciated this respect for our home.

Once in a while a few girls would stay overnight. I remember one incident when two girls stayed over and I found them sleeping in Andy's room with him. After the girls left, I told Andy this behavior was not acceptable. He claimed the girls were just friends, and they may well have been, but Mike and I could not condone this 'modern' attitude. The girls could not stay in the bedroom with Andy; if they wanted to stay they could 'crash' in the Arizona room.

I tried to stop the kids from drinking beer, and would give them lectures on the dangers of drinking, but they would simply smile and listen politely. After I went to bed the kids would bring in the beer and watch television and talk. Andy was drinking beer often, and smoking. He was nervous all the time and had great difficulty sleeping. He could not sleep before one or two o'clock in the morning, and then would sleep late into the day.

During these years there were several sad events that happened to some of Andy's friends. One of the boys from the rice-stealing episode somehow shot himself in the head. He survived but suffered severe brain damage and was paralyzed. The shooting situation was never clear as to whether he was trying to commit suicide or simply playing with the gun. He was a pleasant Hispanic boy with a promising future and we liked him. Six months after the shooting I saw him in church with his mother. He was paralyzed and in a wheelchair. He continues to have serious brain damage and little hope of recovering his mental or physical faculties.

A year later, two of Andy's friends were involved in a car accident. The boy in the passenger seat died of heart failure according to police reports. The other boy, the driver, was found guilty of manslaughter and given a seven-year prison sentence. The boy who died of a heart attack had a history of heart disease and apparently used drugs as well as alcohol. Supposedly, the two of them left a party where Andy was present to buy more beer, when they ran a stop sign and were hit broadside by another vehicle. No one in the second vehicle was injured. Andy and the kids had to give a deposition in the case but were unable to prevent their friend from being sent to prison.

Six months before Andy died another boy whom Andy knew from St. Francis was killed. The boy was with friends in a hotel room after their prom and had taken a gun with him to the party. He was apparently handling the gun when the gun discharged and the bullet struck him in the head. He died at the scene. He was the eldest of a large family, and the family was devastated. I attended his funeral, and six months later, his mother was at my son's funeral. What a heartbreaking world this is, in which we live.

Andy made friends wherever he went. He would then bring these friends home. He loved his home and felt safe there. He took care of his friends, placing their needs before his own. Sometimes we worried about the type of friends he was bringing home, but did not want to be snobs and were glad that Andy brought them to our house. He had friends of every ethnic and socioeconomic background. I suspect that having friends who were less fortunate helped Andy feel better about himself. He felt compelled to help people in need.

Every time Mike and I would go out of town Andy would throw a big party at our house. We did not go out of town very often, but reached a point when we were afraid to leave Phoenix for fear of what would happen at our home. The kids would clean up after their party, but we could tell by the sticky floors and beer cans in the garbage that a party had taken place. If they were trying to be sneaky about the party they failed miserably. In discussions with Andy about the incidents he would flash his engaging smile and promise no more parties. I could never stay mad at Andy when he gave me that look, few people could. Andy knew how to work his smile.

After giving Andy a second chance, we soon went out of town and he threw another party. I asked Andy's friend Tim if his older brother would come over and supervise the boys the next time we were out of town. Tim's brother promised that there would be no kids in the house, and we offered to pay him for his time. Years later, Tim admitted there had been no kids in the house that weekend, but plenty of them were in the 'backyard' at the party. Each time one of the parties happened I would lecture Andy and explain why he should not have kids at the house while we were gone. As usual, he would always listen politely, and then the next time we were gone, have a party. As he matured, he did stop having such large parties and started simply having a few friends over when we were gone. We only went out of town about twice a year without Andy, so the parties were not as frequent as they may seem in retrospect.

This was the time of wild parties for Andy and hanging out with friends on the fringe of society. Andy was going through cars like they were toys. He treated his cars roughly, causing constant trips to the shop for repairs. Mike was furious at the cost for auto repairs, and the mechanics just kept raking in money. Andy and Mike's relationship continued to deteriorate; with me in the middle trying to keep the peace and save my son and my marriage.

Mike's business partnership went through a financial setback that caused him to worry about supporting the family and saving our home. I was in group counseling, which helped me keep going. The women in the group gave me moral support and gave me a safe place to express my feelings and disappointments. They kept reassuring me that Andy would eventually mature.

After Andy's short-lived security guard job, I harassed him into sitting for his General Equivalency Diploma (GED). I was confident he could pass the test without doing any review. I picked up the application, paid the fee and set the time for the test. He fussed and stalled, but took the test. He passed easily and received his GED. With his GED I talked him into going to community college, in return, we would pay for his education and car. He would carry a minimum of twelve credits which would make him a full-time student, and Mike could then keep him on our health insurance plan.

Andy started out with good intentions, but friends needing him constantly interfered with classes and homework. He ended up dropping out of school before the end of semester. Again, my pleading and nagging were a waste of time. The demands of his friends were more important than his personal life and family.

Andy was always riding to the rescue of his friends. Someone in trouble would call and Andy would jump into his car and away he would go. Andy had mistreated the Firebird so badly I thought if he had a nicer car, he might take more pride in ownership, and take better care of the car. Against Mike's wishes, but with his consent, I found a late model burgundy Mustang for Andy. He was excited, and loved his new car, but before long this car was in the shop for repairs. He had no idea how to take care of a car. I do not really know how he could when we paid the expenses. Mike was not mechanically inclined, so we always took the cars to a mechanic for repairs. Mike and I kept our own vehicles as long as possible, making sure regular maintenance was performed as required. Spending money on a new car was not something either of us cared to do.

After he received a few more speeding tickets, Andy's driver's license was in jeopardy again. The insurance companies did not want to insure him, and we were running out of money paying for the repairs to his cars and his fines. The Mustang had to go, so once again mom came to the rescue. I found a red CJ-7 model Jeep and sold the Mustang and bought the Jeep. Supposedly, Andy could not go as fast in the Jeep, and the Jeep would be sturdier than the Mustang. The Jeep was the vehicle Andy owned the longest. He did manage to damage the Jeep quite a few times, going through a clutch, brakes and other assorted parts.

As Andy matured, he did improve in his driving. His driving record became cleaner, with fewer tickets, and he did not have any more car accidents. Andy's old friends from childhood started coming around more, and some of the fringe friends stopped coming around the house. Although Andy's behavior was improving, as were his friends, I continued to caution him about drinking and the history of problems in our family. He admitted he drank beer often when he was sixteen, but said he was now drinking less.

Andy loved going down to Mexico to a beach town called Rocky Point, a favorite party place for many of the young people in Phoenix. I would never let him take his Jeep for fear the car would break down and he would be stranded. One time the boys talked another friend, John, into taking his Jeep to Rocky Point. The Jeep broke down and Andy and his friend had to hitchhike home. The road to Rocky Point is much traveled by Arizona youths and Andy and John soon found a ride to Phoenix. Later in the week I drove John back to pick up his vehicle. Fortunately, his Jeep was still there, and intact.

All of Andy's friends liked me and would talk with me quite freely. The girls were less open with me than the boys. The young people knew I was a soft touch, being kind and caring to them. There was always food for them in a big freezer in the backroom. Andy continued to bring his buddies home, and they would raid the refrigerator and watch television in the

Arizona room. A year after Greg moved out Andy met Brian and Chad, and became friends with them. I think he met them at a bar, but I am not sure. Andy was still not twenty-one, but had no trouble being served in a bar, or buying liquor. A local dive here in Phoenix was the place the guys liked to drink beer and shoot pool.

Brian was a small, skinny young man with a real drinking problem. Andy took him under his wing and drove Brian everywhere. Brian's license had been suspended and he had thousands of dollars in fines pending. Brian took Greg's place, first sleeping on the floor in Andy's room, and later crashing on the sofa in the Arizona room. Brian, like Greg, never caused any problems and asked for nothing except a place to sleep. At first, I worried about Brian, he looked unsavory, with his tangled long dark hair and dark brooding eyes. His eyes were like those of a wounded puppy, and I could never detect any evil in them. Other adults would see him and tell me that he should leave, but I assured them he was harmless.

Brian, as a teenager had married and was the father of two sons. He was very bright and did extremely well in his early married years, making fifty or sixty thousand dollars a year in the landscaping business. He and his wife soon started using drugs and lost everything they owned. Brian and his wife divorced, and his parents took the children into their home. He went to a rehabilitation clinic, but his ex-wife would not stop using drugs. Brian quit using hard drugs but alcohol then became his addiction. Andy would take Brian every Sunday to see his two sons. Against my wishes, Andy would sometimes let Brian take his Jeep on Sundays so he could spend time with his two boys, who were about four and five years old at the time. To Andy, Brian spending time with the children was important. A few times Brian brought the boys to swim at our home. They were nice little boys. We felt sorry for them having divorced parents who could not provide for them. One of the few times Andy talked with me about a future was to tell me that when he had kids he would make sure he spent time with his children doing things together.

Brian tried to repay us for allowing him to stay in our home by trimming our palm trees. He worked as a tree trimmer and was hoping to one day be an arboreal expert. He was no longer staying with us when Andy died, but has been one of Andy's most loyal friends in coming over on Mother's Day or Christmas, and dropping off a small gift. Brian came to visit Mike and me after Andy died, and told us Andy had been the best friend he had ever known. Andy was always there for him and Brian had never known that kind of selfless friendship. I gave Brian Andy's St. Andrew's medal to remember him. Andy often wore the medal around his neck, although he did not have the medal on the night he died.

For many years, girls had come and gone around our house, too numerous to count. Andy drew girls to him like a magnet, some of them nice and some of them not so nice. Andy never attended his own prom, but he certainly attended every other prom. In 1991 and 1992 he must have taken three different girls each year to their Christmas dances and proms. There are some wonderful pictures of him dressed in his tuxedo, looking handsome. I thank God for all the pictures we have of him.

For his girl friend Jamie's Christmas dance one year at Xavier, Andy wore a tuxedo jacket with tuxedo shorts, and tennis shoes. The school dance sponsors gave an award for the most clever attire and Andy won the award. The funny thing was that the shorts were wool, and Andy could not stand the feel of the wool on his legs and hips. He fussed and squirmed while I fixed his cummerbund. I suggested he wear boxer underwear rather than his usual jockey shorts. He was in a hurry to get to Jamie's house, so he did not have time to change. When he arrived at Jamie's house she gave him a pair of her boxer shorts to wear. The girls at this time were wearing boys' boxer shorts as regular shorts. I had to laugh when he told me he wore Jamie's shorts to the dance.

Andy had many very nice girls interested in him, but he seemed to prefer the more neurotic types. I found 'girlie' magazines in his room and asked his father to tell him to get rid of the magazines. Andy threw some of the magazines away but more would find their way into his room. I tried to talk with Andy about how these magazines exploit women, and he would nod his head in agreement, and keep them anyway. Mike and I would not even have the movie channels on cable in the house, because of the access to explicit movies. We tried to teach him moral values about sexuality, but the girls were available and easy. There was one more inappropriate situation, three years after the first, where Mike came home one afternoon to find Andy in bed with his latest girl friend. The girl was embarrassed and Andy was angry and defensive.

Another of Andy's girl friends was extremely high-strung, and tried to kill herself by jumping out of Andy's Jeep as he was driving down the street. Andy stopped her from jumping. However, the last night of his life he telephoned her to say 'goodbye'; she was not home and he left a message on her answering machine which she was never able to return.

At the funeral, when she and her mother asked if there was anything they could do for me I told her she could do me and Andy a favor by getting her life on track. I sincerely hope she has done so and is well and happy today.

"Suicide ranks as the third leading cause of death for young people (behind only accidents and homicide). For those ages 15-19, suicide is the second leading cause of death. Every hour and forty minutes a person under the age of twenty-five completes suicide."

'AAS 1997'

ANDY, WHY DID YOU HAVE TO GO?

*"What lies behind us and what lies before us
are tiny matters, compared to what lies within us."*

Ralph Waldo Emerson

[8]

Making Choices

Reflecting on the choices Andy made in his life, and the choices Mike and I made, the view is much clearer now than at the time we were making decisions. The phrase 'the road to hell is paved with good intentions', could easily be rephrased as 'the road to hell is paved with our choices'. At the time one is making a choice regarding an issue the logic seems rational. Only in retrospect can one see whether the choices were good or bad. I could easily review this manuscript and examine the choices the three of us made which have brought us to this tragic end. The journey into the past will show us where our choices were wrong or misguided, but not what choices would have avoided Andy's death. We can only guess that if we had made another choice the end would have been different.

Some people believe our lives are already set when we come into this world and believe God knows the hour and way of our death. Others believe we have free will, and the ability to direct our fate. I honestly do not know. Since Andy's death I have searched for the answers in a variety of ways, through prayer, through counseling, through reading about death and life after death. Also, I did discover how little has been written about suicide and found even less in the way of comfort for survivors of a suicide. I read many books while trying to make some sense out of Andy's death. I could not believe God wanted Andy to kill himself. What kind of God would permit our beloved son to die simply to teach Mike and me a lesson? Reading the book, *When Bad Things Happen to Good People*, by Harold Kushner, made the most sense to me regarding what happened to Andy, Mike and me. I will reflect more on Dr. Kushner's conclusions in the following chapter. Right now, I would like to review family choices that helped bring us to an ill fated conclusion.

The first important mistake in choice was made by me. Mike and I came to understand early that we had a very sensitive child on our hands. Andy's inability to deal with frustration, and his passive nature were a concern to us. Andy would simply give up and not try to overcome an obstacle that confused him. I remember when he started crawling, he crawled under his high chair, and then did not know how to get out from under the chair. I tried to coax him out and show him how to come around the way he had crawled under the chair. He just sat there and cried. I gave in and helped him from under the chair.

When Andy was six months old, if he was upset about something he would start vomiting. To prevent Andy's suffering I adopted the attitude that life was going to be frustrating enough, and tried to protect him from experiencing frustration and confusion. I realize now I should have worked with him more and somehow taught him to learn to deal with frustrations and problems early in life. By making the choice not to insist that he resolve his problems, a pattern was set early in his life. We will never know if a more skilled parent could have taught Andy to deal with his frustration, we can only assume. Of necessity, as Andy grew older I became more knowledgeable about child development and parenting. As every mother learns, practice is the teacher.

The next choice that might have altered the course of Andy's life was our move to South Bend and, subsequently, to Phoenix. We lived in San Francisco in a pleasant neighborhood near the zoo. I had made friends with other mothers and was learning to be a parent along with them. When the time came for Andy to start grade school he would have attended a small parochial school in the neighborhood. In high school he would have attended a Catholic school also in the neighborhood. This is assuming that we continued to live in San Francisco.

Mike and I had talked about moving to the suburbs. The area we lived in near the ocean had constant fog and I found the weather depressing. Not many children lived in our neighborhood and most of our neighbors were elderly. None of the people we knew had young children, and we questioned whether the city was a good place for a child to grow. I had only the few mothers at preschool to relate to, and no family nearby to give us moral support. With these questions in our minds when the issue of moving to South Bend came up, Mike and I felt we were ready to make a change.

In retrospect I wish we had remained in San Francisco. Perhaps, I would have obtained the letters of recommendation needed to return to college and earn my teaching certificate. In the process maybe I would have learned to be a more effective parent. If I had felt better about myself I probably would not have developed a drinking problem.

By moving to South Bend, I put myself in a situation where I felt less competent in making decisions. In my mind I could not measure up to the religious image of wife and mother the charismatic community encouraged. The year in South Bend was depressing and frustrating for me. The thought occurred to leave Mike, who was thriving in the charismatic community and in his new job. I even considered letting Mike have Andy if I left, because of feeling like such an inadequate wife and mother. I knew that Mike would be too busy with community and working to take care of Andy and that Andy would be left for others to raise. I did not want that to happen. Andy was too dear to me.

South Bend had a record-breaking amount of snow that year in 1977, and we did not see the ground for five months. This weather forced Andy to be indoors more and he learned to watch television during this time. I was continuously depressed and increased the drinking. Mike was never home and I felt isolated and neglected. Eventually, Mike became convinced we could not continue living the way we were and we decided to move to Phoenix.

The next critical choice we made was whether to send Andy to Catholic school or public school. Mike wanted to send him to parochial school because of the religious training. I was not sure Andy should attend parochial school because we lived in an area where the public school district had an excellent reputation. However, within a few years I became disillusioned with the elementary school Andy was attending and we switched him to the Catholic school system.

Questions? If we had sent Andy to parochial school from the very beginning would he have had better success? If we had kept him out of school until he was a year older would he have done better? If we had kept Andy in the public school system would he have been better off? We will never know. We can only make guesses. Did what happen to Andy in school make a difference in his life? I think his experiences in school made an important difference. Andy started school a bright happy child, eager and excited, but anxious. By the time he was in the third grade he was developing headaches and stomach problems, finding any excuse to be sick and stay home from school. He was often sick with colds and bronchial problems. His negative experiences in elementary school severely damaged his self-esteem.

Mike's choice to focus on his career and leave me to raise Andy was a crucial decision for the family. I needed help raising Andy and Mike was seldom there for us. I was responsible for managing our home, rearing Andy, and taking care of Mike's needs. Mike never even bought his own shoes until after Andy died. I did literally everything for the family and tried to work part-time as well. I thought this was the price to pay to be a stay-at-home mom. Andy needed his father to be involved in his daily life. Mike did not like the way I was indulging Andy by being permissive, but he was not willing to work on a better way. After Andy turned five, Mike rarely did anything with him without me along. I begged and pleaded for Mike to do more 'guy' things with Andy, but he could not see the need. His father had never done those things with him and he could not see why doing things with his son was important.

If Mike had created a different relationship with his son, would the end have been different? Andy felt his father never approved of him and thought he could never measure up to his father's expectations. I know this because when Andy was older he told me. I think Andy's lack of self-worth began with a little boy wondering why his father never played with him or spent time with him. I have learned through studying psychology that children blame themselves for their parents' actions. Abused children love and defend their abuser, i.e., blaming themselves for causing the parent to hit them. If a child thinks a parent does not love them the child believes the lack of love is because they, the children, are unlovable. I am sure having his father take a more active role in Andy's life would have helped, but would this one factor have changed the course of his life? I doubt that the answer is simple.

Andy enjoyed the martial arts class we all started when he was about ten years old. If he had continued with martial arts would he have learned the self-control he lacked? I tried to get him to return to the program when he was in his teens, paying for a lifetime membership in a local gym. Andy went a few times, and then refused to go anymore, saying he did not like the instructor. I bought Andy books on martial arts, several about the actor Bruce Lee whom he admired.

The next important choice we made which may have been a factor was to allow Andy to attend Brophy. Andy really was not Brophy material, academically or emotionally. He was not a serious student, preferring to have fun and socialize with his friends. He also was not aware of academic and social differences in people. We raised Andy to believe that everyone is created equally and no one is made more important because of their money, parents, home or car. In fairness to Brophy, few of the young men who attend the school have a superior attitude.

The reality is there are individuals in every facet of life who think money, position, family or fame makes them better than other people. Most of Andy's friends did not fit into the elitist category, although they seemed to hold themselves in high esteem. I think Andy was simply left behind in the crowd. His friends were busy adapting and doing well and they forgot him. Brophy is a much larger school than Andy was accustomed to attending and the atmosphere was more reserved. He probably would have been better off at St. Mary's. We will never know. Based on the above scenario Andy apparently chose not to fit in at Brophy after his first year there.

Another consideration, once Mike and I saw how reckless Andy was driving his car we probably should have taken away his driver's license. Perhaps, as he gained more social experience he might have developed a more mature attitude toward driving and the responsibility of owning a car. Once a young man has a driver's license, taking away the license is more traumatic than simply never allowing him to have the license. Until Andy turned sixteen and was going through puberty, his behavior was not reckless or irresponsible. He had always been a cautious child, rarely getting into disagreements or fights. Other than the fact that we could not get him to apply himself at school, in most situations, he was a pleasant companion.

Andy's choice to leave the scene when he hit a fence post in the Pontiac Firebird accident set many negative consequences in motion. He did not leave the scene because he was afraid of what would happen to him. He left the scene because he was in a hurry to get to Jamie's house and make up with her. I doubt he knew or even thought about the consequences of leaving the scene of the accident.

Maybe, with Andy's temperament, being an only child was difficult for him. My choice not to have any more children resulted in Andy growing up alone, with no siblings to learn how to share and exchange confidences. As a matter of fact, there were no 'grownups' for him to talk with or to encourage him; the only adult in his life was me. My parents died when Andy was eight years old and Mike's parents died two years later. Neither set of grandparents was ever involved with Andy in any way, so he did not have the benefit of their love and comfort. Andy's aunts and uncles were busy with their own children, and the families had no time to include him. The family gatherings at holidays were the only times the relatives were together. Over the years Andy spent time with his cousins, David and Shawn. Sometimes the brothers would go with us on our vacations to San Diego, and sometimes Andy would stay with them when Mike and I went out of town. Looking into the past I find no adult, young or old, who spent time with Andy or was available to him. Would the influence of other adults have benefitted Andy? Probably, but none were available; so much for the benefit of being around extended family.

Once Andy started driving the three of us seemed to lose perspective. Andy exercised no self-control or sense of responsibility about anything. I kept running to the rescue and Mike kept complaining about the cost. Andy's choices in friends became very questionable. Many of the young people who came through our home were walking on the wild side and Andy followed along with them. Andy put his friends' needs above his own and I believe many of them used Andy as a chauffeur and a scapegoat. They took advantage of his good nature and let him take all the consequences for their behavior. Most of them had no money, and Andy paid for the gas, provided the car and took risks by drinking and driving.

Now we know that we should have taken the car and license away from him after the third car accident, even though none of the accidents were legally his fault. I really think, by then, Andy was already on a path to self-destruction. After he died, some of his friends told me when Andy was sixteen he held a gun to his head and talked about shooting himself. I do not know why he held a gun to his head; the boys seemed to think he really was not serious about killing himself. They dismissed the incident as simply Andy liking to 'walk on the edge', tempting fate.

Andy always seemed to make questionable choices in life.

Situations never went smoothly for him for more than three months. I know this sounds like a peculiar observation, but I noticed a pattern of behavior a year or so before he died. He would start school, a new job, a new relationship, and within three months all hell would break loose, and his life would be in chaos.

One time, Andy chose to drive for three months on a suspended license I did not know was suspended. After the suspension was removed, the police stopped him for speeding and his license was taken away because he had not filed the paper work to have his license reinstated. Only then did I find out about the original license suspension for too many speeding tickets. I decided to bail him out of trouble and not let him suffer the consequences of being unable to drive for six months. A mistake, but again, I am not sure he would not have killed himself then. The thought of not being able to drive was terrifying for Andy. The freedom he felt while driving may be the one thing that kept him going.

When he turned seventeen, and was a junior at Brophy, Andy chose to go through Catholic confirmation. We gave him the choice, because by now we had to plead with him to go to church with us on Sundays. I am not certain he chose to be confirmed because he wanted God in his life, or because his friends from Brophy were going through confirmation; maybe there was a little of both. I suspect Andy wanted help and hoped God would give him the support that none of the people in his life were offering him. Unfortunately, God does not work that way. If God did, Andy would have been helped long before, because his father and I prayed daily for help and guidance for him.

Mike and I always talked about *when* Andy went to college, not *if* he went to college. Andy never talked about college or a future. Even when he was a little boy he had no interest in being a grownup. He liked being a child, and told me when he was a teenager that he never wanted to become an adult. However, some decisions had to be made about his future. Math came to him easily, and he exhibited some natural talent when he took an art class at a vocational school after dropping out of Central. Andy had excellent visual spatial ability.

Mike's Irish grandfather was an artist, and his youngest sister and a niece were artists, suggesting that creativity runs in the family. Andy began his paintings when he was nineteen and going to vocational school to receive his credits to graduate from high school. The paintings were of objects depicting pain and suffering. A psychiatrist would probably have a field day interpreting and diagnosing the meaning behind his paintings.

By not completing high school Andy could not attend a university. Mike and I were community college graduates and believe the community college an excellent choice to complete the first two years of college before going to a university. The tuition is also more reasonable. Although Andy dropped out of high school I continued to encourage him to go to college. He started college two different times, but simply could not apply himself, choosing to spend time with his friends rather than attend classes. Andy told me he felt abandoned when his friends from Brophy left for college. I told him he could not enroll in a university until he improved his grades through the community college system. His Brophy and St. Francis friends came around when they were home from college to party with him.

However, when the time came the friends returned to college and forgot about Andy until the next time they were home. The choice not to continue in college was Andy's. I tried every argument to get him to realize he needed an education. He enjoyed the good life and a low-paying job was not going to meet his needs. I truly thought a few years in the work force and more maturity would make him see the importance of an education; that he would return to school and apply himself. I still think he would have come to the decision to return to college, but now he will never have the chance.

I am convinced Andy suffered from clinical depression. No one saw the depression but me. I was the only person who heard his crying and saw the lack of energy and lack of interest in his daily life. However, when one of his friends called he became all smiles and laughter. He was either with someone or on the phone all of his waking hours. Somehow he could not function alone. He went from being a little boy who could play by himself for hours to a young man who was only happy when others were around, the more the merrier. There was never an uninterrupted conversation with him before the phone rang or a friend came over.

In my opinion, there is little question that Andy's depression was due to a chemical imbalance in his brain. My reasoning for thinking he suffered from depression was the dramatic change in his personality between childhood and adolescence. A true Jekyll and Hyde transformation occurred when Andy started puberty. Another factor to consider is that I suffer from depression and believe members of Mike's family also have a history of depression. Andy refused to allow me to get him professional help. When he was sixteen we forced him to go to counseling for three months, and then he wanted to quit. When he was nineteen he could not sleep and suffered from stomach pains. My thought was that if a psychiatrist prescribed antidepressants for Andy the medicine might offer him some comfort.

I selected a psychiatrist who was recommended to me by a

friend and coaxed Andy into an appointment. The psychiatrist wrote Andy two prescriptions: an ulcer medicine and a muscle relaxant. Andy's stomach pain turned out to be an ulcer; at nineteen years of age. He saw the psychiatrist two more times and then refused to go, saying the psychiatrist could not even remember his name. Andy also said talking about his problems only made him cry and did not solve his problems. Another factor, if the doctor had been more interested in Andy would the therapy have continued? Would antidepressants have helped? Questions I can never answer because the psychiatrist chose to ignore my suggestion for antidepressants and gave Andy muscle relaxants instead. The muscle relaxants did not help either.

After Andy gave up on college, he decided he was going to volunteer for the Marine Corps. He talked to recruiters and was planning to enlist. During the physical exam the medics discovered the ulcer. The Marines would not take him until the ulcer was cured. Andy began to think he might like to be a drug enforcement agent. He liked the idea of the excitement and catching bad guys. How he was going to become a drug enforcement agent I do not know. The military might have provided one avenue of maturity, but with an ulcer the chances of his acceptance into the military were nonexistent. Andy's ulcer never improved as he would change none of his eating or drinking habits to relieve the condition.

The year before Andy died, he seemed to be maturing and developing a sense of responsibility. He was not as happy as he had been, we did not hear his boisterous laughter as much, but the emotional lows were not as severe. Andy even suggested he might help his father and me with our youth church confirmation group in the Fall. The previous two years Mike and I had been part of a youth instructional team helping prepare young people for confirmation into the Catholic church. We were very pleased when Andy suggested on his own that he might help us with the classes. Andy had drifted completely away from the church. The last time he attended church was for midnight mass the Christmas before he died. He had promised me he would go to Easter mass with us, but when the time came he refused to attend. I remember, because I was so disappointed. Mike and I attended mass at Brophy Chapel for Easter services and Andy's buddies were there with their parents. Everyone asked where he was and I had to tell them he would not wake up to come to church. The boys laughed and said, "that's Andy."

The girls Andy chose to care about were another nightmare. There were dozens of girls coming through our house during those years, and he always managed to date the most neurotic. The girls who seemed to have their heads on straight Andy thought of as friends, the ones who exhibited problems were his choice. His first love lasted about two years before they separated. She continued to be a friend and a few weeks before he killed himself the two of them drove to Los Angeles for a long weekend with some friends of hers. He said he had a good time, but I noticed the light had gone out of his eyes. We have a photograph taken when they were dressed in old western costumes. Andy dressed as a cowboy with a rifle in his hands; she is sitting on a saloon bar dressed as a dance-hall girl. In the photograph Andy appears sad.

I believe he could have decided to kill himself after his twenty-first birthday was such a disappointing event. He thought his friends would throw him a big birthday party, but they did not. Mike and I went out of town on the weekend of his birthday, and the house was still in one piece when we came home. I had asked Andy if he wanted me to plan a party and he said 'no', but now I wish we had celebrated his twenty-first birthday. On reflection, I think Andy never admitted his disappointment when positive things did not happen for him.

Andy had a very catastrophic way of looking at situations and events. Whenever any incident out of the ordinary happened he took the most negative point of view. For example, he told friends in high school that his father beat him. Mike had given him a few light swats before the age of ten. Andy was convinced his father would throw him out of the house, yet his father never mentioned throwing him out of the house. We never made this threat. In spite of all the parties and people in our house at all hours of the day and night, we never considered asking Andy to leave home. Andy appeared to be a pessimist. He expected the worst, even when no basis was there for him to think the worst.

He cared about several young women at different times, but because he had a tendency to flirt they were jealous and moody. Young women liked Andy, and I guess he had difficulty being faithful to just one. I think many of the young men envied the success Andy had with girls and liked to be around to catch the fallout he left behind. I do not know where he learned to treat women with so little respect. His father and I always tried to treat each other with respect. Andy never hit a young lady, though several of them attacked him, and he had a small scar on his face as proof.

Another issue became his love of guns. He always managed to borrow a gun from someone so he could go into the desert and shoot. I would never permit a firearm to remain in the house. Somehow I had a fear, maybe a precognition, of guns. If I found a gun in the house, I would confiscate the gun and make Andy return the weapon to the owner. Andy and some of his friends from Brophy went into the desert and had paint gun wars; these guns shoot paint pellets to score a 'hit'. In fact, we have an interesting picture of Andy, Richard and Jason in the desert wearing their camouflage with paint guns under their arms. I think Tim was the cameraman. Andy really enjoyed these games, especially if Richard was involved. They rented the paint guns and bought the paint balls at gun stores.

The handgun Andy used to kill himself was left with him by a friend who went on vacation. Andy kept the gun in his car because he knew if I found the firearm I would take the weapon for 'safekeeping'. The handgun was a nine-millimeter semiautomatic. The last month of Andy's life I lived in a premonition of fear. I knew something terrible was about to happen, but did not know what the 'something' was. Andy told Tim that I knew he had the gun in his car and was okay with his having the gun. Nothing could have been further from the truth and Andy knew this.

Three weeks before Andy died, he came home from work and told me he did not want to live, but that he would not take his own life. I tried to talk with him about what he was feeling. However, during the conversation, the telephone rang and he was off and running on another errand. I continued to worry about our conversation and what he had told me. I prayed daily for Andy, but then one day made a peculiar choice: I gave Andy to God. Andy had been the center of my prayers all his life. I was still asking God to help Andy, and if this meant the only way Andy could know joy and peace again was to be with God, then I would let him go. Let God's will, not mine, be done. Was I keeping Andy alive by my prayers, did he die because I let go? My emotional self believes that I kept him alive the last five years through my perseverance and prayer. Another part of me told me that I should have taken some action immediately after Andy said he did not want to live. I was going to do something, but decided to wait and see if he received his promotion as a courier for an attorney's office. The promotion might have been a positive factor and improved his attitude. Andy seemed to be maturing. I was planning to insist he have a complete physical exam and try to get him on medication for depression. My hope was that success at work would interest him and his life would improve. Now, of course, I realize action should have been taken immediately; even if that meant committing him to a hospital.

There is no certainty that committing someone to a mental hospital is always the answer. As a matter of procedure, hospitals medicate patients, and when the patients say they feel better the doctors allow them to go home. Andy was an expert at making people believe he was okay. I should know; I am an expert too. Few people suspect that I suffer from depression. Since his death my depression stays with me like an old friend who enjoys making my life miserable. In all probability, my depression in the past was biochemical; however, I believe my current depression is situational, caused by the death of my only child.

I do not know if Andy's death was inevitable or truly preventable. Maybe factors were set in place long ago that could not be altered, or did we really have choices, and simply kept making the wrong decisions. The experts on suicide say Andy had a choice, and he chose. I disagree. When a person is so depressed they see no reason to live, they are unable to make choices. The choice the person does make may be the 'only choice' available to them at the time.

Iris Bolton in her book on the suicide of her son, *My Son, My Son*, tells how her son walked by his father and his father's friend who were talking at the kitchen table. He then went to his bedroom where he called his girl friend and while talking to her on the telephone shot himself. I believe at the time a person is getting ready to commit suicide they are in a state of 'zoning'. The term is used in sports when an athlete seems to be in a hypnotic state, unable to make an error in their performance. I believe Andy was in a 'zone' when he killed himself. After returning home from the precinct, he went into his room, then out again, walking past his cat and our dog sleeping on his bed; past my bedroom where the door was partly open; he then took a taxi to where the police had stopped him in his car and drove home.

At home he tried to call his girl friend and then intentionally, or unintentionally, shot himself. I do not believe he knew what he was doing, or the chaos he would leave behind. I believe the idea that the person committing suicide has made a willing choice is about as accurate as the idea that a person willingly develops cancer. I am not willing to absolve myself of guilt by believing Andy had a 'choice'.

> *"People who drink alcohol in addition to being depressed are at a greater risk for suicide. Four times as many men kill themselves as do women. Firearms are the most common method of suicide among all groups."*
>
> *'AAS'*

ANDY, WHY DID YOU HAVE TO GO?

"Look and you will find it —
what is unsought will go undetected."

Sophocles

[9]

Survival: The Following Years

If one never believed in God before, surviving the loss of an only child will take you to the altar of God. An alternative to turning toward God is to die. The death is a spiritual one, where one becomes bitter and angry at the world. A person becomes full of resentment and jealousy toward those who have not had to walk through this heartbreak.

The night Andy died, Mike and I turned toward each other and God. We promised each other we would walk together the pain and loss of Andy. Mike and I have very different personalities, and we each handle our grief in different ways. I was not sure our marriage would survive the loss of Andy. The rate of divorce after the death of a child is extremely high, about 80 percent according to health care statistics. I have seen no pertinent figures, but I feel that the rate of divorce following the suicide of a child must be even higher. More than four years have passed since Andy's death, and Mike and I are closer than ever. I cannot say we will never be divorced. The future is unknown. All we have is this day and this moment, and all else is fortune telling. There is no question that Mike and I would change the past if we could bring back our son, but we cannot. We have learned so much about ourselves, and relationships in these years since Andy's death. We both share the guilt in failing our son, but we have never blamed each other.

The days following Andy's death are vague to me. The doctors pronounced him dead at 5:00 a.m., Thursday, August 4, 1994. We held the memorial service the following Saturday evening at 7:00 p.m. at St. Francis Xavier Church, where Andy had received communion, served as an altar boy and was confirmed as a Catholic. Only two days had passed since Andy's death, and we did not think many people would have heard about Andy dying. Andy's friend Tim had called their closest friends, who called still more of Andy's friends, and about two hundred young people came to the service. Another three hundred people present were friends of Andy, Mike and me.

After the funeral, Mike and I felt we needed time to ourselves, and decided to make a trip up the coast of California on our way to Washington to see my stepfather. We would stop in Fresno to see my sister and then continue up the coast to Oregon. One of Mike's friends, Rick Karber, and his wife owned a cabin in Oregon and gave us the keys. We planned to stay at the cabin for a few days, then continue to Washington.

Mike and I had several tasks to resolve before we could leave Phoenix. Friends and associates were kind and supportive. In my mind, the first thing that needed to be taken care of was getting rid of the couch and carpet where Andy had died. The couch where Andy had been sitting and the carpet where the paramedics had laid Andy were covered with blood, and a terrible sight for anyone to see. I never went back into the room after the paramedics came and attended Andy, until the scene was cleaned. We will forever be in debt to my brother-in-law Bill, Peggy's husband. He is a retired paramedic, and had seen these scenes before as part of his job. Peggy called Bill and asked him if he knew someone who could come to dispose of the couch and carpet. Bill arranged to come with another man in a truck Thursday, the day Andy died, to take the couch and carpet away.

I was still in shock and walked through events on autopilot; making arrangements for someone to look after the house while Mike and I were on the trip. My employers at the college were told that I would not finish teaching my summer classes. They later told me how surprised they were at my matter-of-fact attitude. The reason for my calm was because my emotions were dead. There was only emptiness.

Mike and I agreed to have Andy's remains cremated. We believe a person's spirit lives on, and the body is an empty vessel, once a person has died. Mike and I had always agreed on cremation after death and decided we wanted the same for our son. Apparently, due to city ordinances, the crematoriums only use the furnaces on certain days; and then the ashes need twenty-four hours to cool. We had to wait three days for the cremation before we could pick up the ashes. We were anxious to begin our trip to Oregon and Washington, because our home was empty and sad without Andy. He and his friends had always filled the house with their laughter and antics. The telephone was always ringing, young people coming and going, and now there was silence.

On our way out of town we drove to the crematorium in Chandler and picked up Andy's ashes. The remains were in a cardboard box which we took with us, not really knowing what to do with them. We discussed sprinkling Andy's remains in San Francisco Bay, but neither of us was ready to dispose of them.

We took books to read and tapes to listen to on our trip; the books and tapes were specifically about death and grieving and trying to understand and accept the death of a loved one. Two tapes we felt helped us were *Embraced by the Light*, by Betty J. Eadie, and *When God Doesn't Make Sense* by Dr. James Dobson. Mike and I were disappointed and surprised when we were unable to find much information about suicide or the survivors of suicide. A friend of mine, who is also a therapist, lent me books by psychic Doris Stokes, an English author. These books gave me the greatest comfort and hope. Stokes had a very positive outlook on life and death, and the continuation of the spirit after death, even if the death was by suicide. The books are out of print, and I was unable to find copies for myself when we returned to Phoenix.

In reading other books written by psychics, they seem less positive about the spirit of a suicide. These books and tapes helped me believe Andy was still with me in spirit. My conviction is that I could not survive without believing one day I will see Andy again and hold him close to my heart and hear his voice. Mike probably feels the same way about Andy, although he has never expressed his thoughts.

Mike and I did not talk much on our trip. We would listen to the tapes by Eadie and Dobson and reflect on what the tapes said to us. Most of the time we were traveling we simply drove down the road and grieved, sometimes crying as we drove, and other times lost in our own thoughts. We wanted desperately to understand the 'how' and 'why' of Andy's death. The world was supposed to make sense and Andy's death did not make sense. God is supposed to be a loving compassionate God, how could He take our beloved son? Mike and I had always tried to be faithful to God. Certainly, we made mistakes and were far from perfect, but we really tried to live according to God's teachings. Mike had always believed that if he were faithful to God, God in turn would keep our son safe. Mike constantly reassured me Andy would be 'all right' and that God would look after Andy. Is suicide God's way of looking after our child? I could have easily gotten mad at God, and turned away during this time. Instead, I looked to God for comfort, and felt He was weeping with me. The poem *Footprints*, by an unknown author, became my prayer.

My belief was that God was carrying me through this valley of darkness, because I could not make the journey alone. Mike has always been more faithful to morning prayer and God. Now Mike had to reexamine his belief about what God would or would not do if one were faithful. My desire was for God to be Santa Claus and give me what I prayed for. When the present was not given my feeling was that God did not love me. The result was to turn away, not spending time in daily prayer. Eventually, my spiritual needs would get the best of me and I would turn back to God, because He was the only power who could help me.

Enroute to Oregon we stopped overnight in Fresno to see my sister Ina. The next day we continued to Oregon. Andy's death has taught us many things, one being that we are truly blessed by having wonderful family and friends.

The cabin in Oregon was an elaborate home set on a beautiful lake surrounded by the mountains. We laughed when we saw the 'cabin'. The house was two stories with three or more bedrooms, completely furnished and ready for occupancy. Our friends, the Karbers, would go to their cabin when their time permitted. They retained a caretaker who kept the house ready for them or guests. Mike and I were able to buy fresh food at the local grocery store for whatever meals we wanted. The cabin faced a peaceful lake where we could sit on the deck and watch boats glide by on the water. The Karbers had a boathouse and several boats which were at our disposal. The lake is very large and beautiful. Mountains surrounded the lake, and there were many homes nestled among the trees along the shoreline. The lake is located near North Bay, but the name of the lake escapes me. I do remember the serene beauty of the lake.

Mike and I rested at the cabin for a few days, sharing memories of Andy. After a few days the solitude began to wear on us and we became restless and moved on to Washington. We did not stay at the cabin as long as planned, but the respite did help quiet our troubled souls. We continued our travel to Washington where my stepfather was waiting anxiously for us. My stepfather, Larue, did not know what to say to us about Andy's death, but was pleased to see us. We never told him about Andy's ashes in the trunk of the car. Perhaps, logically there is no explanation, but having Andy's remains with us was comforting. Somehow, he was making the trip with us, his spirit keeping us company.

My stepfather is a quiet man like my husband. Their kind of quietness is comforting. Words do not always have to be spoken for someone to convey love and concern. There are no words at a time like this anyway, but most people do not have the sense to know this and continue to talk. Mike and I took long walks on the spit near my stepfather's house in Sequim. The small community is located on the Olympic Peninsula north of Seattle. The area has many lovely towns resting on the shores. The spit is a long narrow strip of land jutting out from the shore with a lighthouse at the end to warn ships of the rocky coast. The point is covered with sand and rocks and pieces of wood that have washed ashore. Some of the wood was large logs, creating an obstacle to climb over before reaching the lighthouse. The walk to the end of the spit is about three miles and a difficult trip. Mike and I walked on the shore often, but never all the way to the lighthouse.

I cannot recall how long we stayed in Sequim, but once again we were restless and ready to return home and face the reality of life without Andy. We were gone from Phoenix three weeks, arriving home the end of August. Mike and I immediately returned to work. Paradise Valley Community College and Ottawa University where I teach part-time offered me a leave of absence, but I needed to work. Teaching is a wonderful outlet for me. I enjoy the students and the course content and my colleagues are pleasant and kind people. Some people were concerned about my returning to work so soon, but I could not allow myself to stay home and mourn, because I was not ready to accept Andy's death. More time needed to pass for me to come to terms with the fact that Andy was really gone.

The reality that Andy was never coming home again took me more than two years to acknowledge. The guilt and the self-loathing were emotions that overwhelmed me during the first few years. I blamed myself completely for having failed Andy. Mike had failed too, but he did not know any better. He had done what he thought was best for Andy. The fact he would never have the relationship with Andy he had dreamed of having would become very painful. On the other hand I am a therapist, and should have anticipated and understood our failures. Andy told me three weeks before he died, he did not want to live, but would not kill himself. If I had listened to my inner voice, God speaking, perhaps I would have been more aggressive in pursuing treatment for him and he might be alive today. But then again, he might not.

If I seem ambivalent, the reason is that perhaps Andy's fate was predetermined when he first came into the world. There are other stories of parents whose children have committed suicide, and many of them say the children made several attempts before succeeding. By interceding, are we parents simply delaying the inevitable? There are many more questions regarding how we can prevent the tragedy of suicide, than answers. Possibly, there are no answers. I only know we survivors must keep trying to prevent this tragic waste of our loved ones. The mental health care professionals give many different theories, but we can never know for sure until we meet our loved one again and they tell us why.

Two months after Andy died our family was dealt another terrible blow when our oldest nephew was struck and killed by lightning. His death brought back to me in a flood all the pain and sorrow of Andy's death. The tragedy of Danny's death made me stop and get back in touch with my pain. I was still not addressing my grief over the loss of Andy. My sister-in-law, Judy, and I now share a common bond: the loss of a young son. Danny was a wonderful young man soon to graduate from the University of Arizona in Tucson with a degree in architecture. Danny's death made no more sense than Andy's, although there was not the stigma of suicide. The family could console themselves with the idea God had called Danny home. Danny's death was an act of God. He had been camping with friends near Tucson. During a summer storm a bolt of lightning traveled through a tree down the root, which was under the tent where Danny and his friends were sitting. The lightning continued through the root to the metal pole supporting the tent, electrocuting Danny. The two other young men in the tent were slightly injured. The boys thought they were safe playing cards in their tent waiting for the storm to pass.

Following this tragedy, I was there to comfort my sister-in-law and her family. The six surviving children were in shock, but they could share their grief. The family asked me to make suggestions for the memorial service. Since they also chose cremation and a simple memorial service, my suggestion was to make a video recording of the service. I realize that making a videotape sounds macabre. Nevertheless, I can remember very little of Andy's memorial service, or the people who attended or the flowers on the altar. My sister-in-law's family made a video and added personal comments by friends about Danny. These comments were a wonderful addition to the video. I would love to have some kind of record from Andy's friends of the fun times they shared.

The first year of Andy's death, Mike and I could not deal with the festivities of Thanksgiving and Christmas holidays. In reality, no one in the family felt much like celebrating the holidays that year. The books and information we received from friends about grieving told us to be kind to ourselves, and do whatever necessary to get through the holidays without torturing ourselves. There were many friends and acquaintances who lived out of state who did not know Andy had died and would be expecting an annual family letter from me. I chose to write a poem about Andy, and made a memorial card with his picture. The poem, with a brief note saying Andy had died, said we would not be celebrating Christmas. However, we were wishing all of them joy and happiness for the coming years. Mike and I made plans to go away for Thanksgiving and Christmas. We drove to Sante Fe for Thanksgiving. We had never been to Santa Fe and people who had visited told us the village was lovely. The weather and scenery were pleasant. In our grief, we could not appreciate the beauty.

In December we flew to New Orleans and Mississippi for the week of Christmas. We had never been to New Orleans, and we enjoy listening to jazz. We also wanted to visit our friends, Ray and Kathy West from Phoenix, who moved to Mississippi the month Andy died. New Orleans was quiet by New

Orleans' standards, and we could sightsee without huge crowds and go to Preservation Hall to listen to jazz. We stayed in New Orleans for Christmas, and then rented a car the day after Christmas and drove to Pheba, Mississippi, near Columbus. Our visit with the Wests was peaceful and pleasant. They had converted a farm into a cattle ranch and visiting them was an enjoyable diversion. Ray and Kathy are good friends and we enjoyed catching up on what was happening in their new life.

When living in Phoenix, Ray had a stressful job as a mortgage broker and Kathy worked with him. Ray was the first person to take Mike horseback riding at a cattle ranch near Prescott, Arizona. Kathy's brother-in-law owned the land. Ray liked the operation so much that he decided to buy his own place. After their three daughters were grown they decided to buy property in Mississippi. When we visited, they were working hard and enjoying their new lifestyle.

Mike and I were very relieved that we had planned to leave Phoenix for the holidays. The pain of Andy's death was always with us, but by being away from the festivities at home at least the pain was not made worse by being reminded Andy would never celebrate another holiday with us. By the time we returned to Phoenix the next school semester was starting for me, and income tax season began for Mike. We were able to resume our work, running to avoid the memories. I wanted to visit a grief counselor and Mike agreed to go with me. He could not see how talking about Andy's death would help, but wanted to be supportive of me. He was finding comfort in daily morning mass and the rosary.

I was finding some relief through my teaching and tennis. Tennis, especially, has been a wonderful activity for me. Only a few of the ladies in my tennis group knew of my loss, and those who did were very kind and did not ask questions. For the short time when playing tennis my focus was on hitting a little yellow ball and forgetting everything else. Sometimes playing with tears in my eyes, but nonetheless playing. Listening to the other women talk about their children and grandchildren was difficult for me. My companions did not know how much their stories reminded me my child was dead, and that I will never know the joys of being a grandmother. Envy occasionally reared an ugly head as I listened to their stories. Occasionally, after the tennis matches I would get into my car and cry all the way home. My feelings were to tell them how fortunate they were and to cherish their children and grandchildren, but I did not want to intrude in their personal lives.

One of the many blessings Mike and I have been given since Andy's death has been his many friends. I run into them wherever I go; sometimes one is a student in my class, or waiting on me at the grocery store or the bank. His closest friends have stayed in touch. Tim went back to college in San Diego after Andy died, but often when he came home for the holidays he would stop by to say hello.

Richard, Andy's dearest friend from grammar school days, went back East to the Merchant Marine Academy after he graduated from high school. Fortunately, he and Andy mended their disagreement before Andy died, and they saw each other not too long before Andy's death. Richard's parents told us he had a salute to Andy engraved on his graduation ring from the academy. Jason was another grammar and high school friend, would call often after Andy's death. He was at the University of Arizona. Often, when Andy was alive, he would drive to Tucson to see Jason on weekends, or they would talk on the telephone. Jason was unable to attend Andy's memorial service because he was in ROTC summer boot camp. I think not being able to be at the memorial service made closure difficult for

Jason. He is an intelligent, reflective young man and Andy's death was a real loss to him. After Andy's death Jason would sometimes telephone us at night to talk. He would be thinking of Andy and need to talk about their times together. He needed to make sense of Andy's death, too.

I invited his calls and enjoyed listening to him talk about Andy. Jason also continues to come to our home occasionally. In fact, he gave us the honor of asking us to be Eucharistic ministers at his wedding. We never expected Andy's friends to stay in touch this long, but they have, and we are grateful. His friends still love him and his memory will always be with them.

Being a family therapist, I found selecting a counselor difficult. One sad commentary: in my search for a therapist to help me deal with my grief I discovered that most grief therapists are incompetent. The first therapist we saw was a nun. She followed the guidelines for the stages in grief, stages with which I was already familiar. She was well-intentioned, but had no clue what pain and questioning parents experience. In my opinion, the natural death of parents and siblings is different from the tragic loss of loved ones through accident, illness, homicide or suicide. The day she could not wait to tell me of an automobile accident, which had claimed the lives of two teenage sisters, was the day we ended our sessions. Hearing of other parents' sorrow was not a comfort to me. Instead, my heart broke again thinking about those poor parents and their pain. This tragedy convinced me even more how unfair life can be.

In my continuing search for help, I located an agency, EMPACT-Suicide Prevention Center, with a counseling program called 'Survivors of Suicide'. 'Survivors of Suicide' is the only support group program in Phoenix for people who suffer the loss of a family member through suicide. Mike was even less enthusiastic about sharing in a group setting, but he went with me. We only attended one session. Interestingly, most of the people there had suffered the loss of either a spouse or a sibling. That particular night we were the only couple there, and the only people who had suffered the loss of a child, and an only child at that. Neither Mike nor I found much comfort in the group sharing, and decided not to continue. However, recently I attended a half-day conference sponsored by EMPACT for 'Survivors of Suicide'. The information was beneficial and perhaps when my teaching schedule permits we may consider attending future group sessions.

Over the past four years I have learned that each person must travel their own personal road to recovery from the loss of a loved one through suicide. As much as Mike and I love one another, we have had to walk the road of sorrow alone. We walk this road knowing the other person is there for us, yet knowing too that our pain is unique to us. Only God truly knows what we are feeling and the pain in our hearts.

Obviously, there is no way for me to know what Mike is feeling as a father in grieving for his son, nor can Mike know my feelings as a mother grieving the loss of my son. The one thing we do share is the knowledge we are both hurting and the pain is forever. Our loss and pain have brought us closer together. Mike finds talking about Andy difficult; for me talking about Andy is difficult, but pleasurable at the same time. Out of respect for Mike, I do not often talk to him about Andy. Out of respect for me, Mike allows me to talk about Andy. Sometimes an incident will remind us of Andy. At those times we do not need words, we know the other is dying inside. And so we simply hold each other in our arms. We understand no words can make our world right again. The only thing that could make our world truly right again is to have Andy back.

Anything less is ash in our mouths.

One day Mike came home from a 'Christians in Commerce' meeting and told me that some of his friends had given him the name of a therapist whom they held in high regard. Anna was a 'Reality Therapist', and this type of therapy was the only approach Mike felt made sense. Years before, we had attended a marriage retreat where the facilitator had been a 'Reality Therapist' and Mike had commented that this program seemed logical to him. We made an appointment to see Anna and discovered we appreciated her methods of therapy. She did not tell us we should not continue to grieve. She gave us ideas to consider, listened attentively and was nonjudgmental. Mike continued the sessions with me for a few months, but he did not feel the need to discuss issues with Anna. My suggestion to him was that he did not have to continue and that was the last time he went.

Through therapy with Anna, and daily prayer for guidance from God, I was beginning to find my way through my pain. She gave me 'true unconditional positive regard' as a human being. She validated me as an individual and was aware of my sorrow. She did not try to minimize or talk me out of my pain. My problem was I did not want to walk through the pain, but wanted the pain to end. Anna accepted my personal grief and I began to develop the courage to live again. I can honestly say she saved my life.

In May 1995 I attended a three-day conference in Phoenix presented by the American Association of Suicidology. In the conference there were stories shared by other suicide survivors. There were also ideas on how to cope with birthdays, anniversaries and holidays of deceased loved ones.

Andy had always liked parties and I felt guilty about not celebrating his twenty-first birthday. So, I decided to give a party for his twenty-second birthday, July 19, 1995. This date would be three weeks before the first anniversary of his death. Mike approved of the birthday party and we told Tim, Andy's friend, of our plan. He thought a party was a great idea since in the past our house was 'the party house'. Tim spread the word and on Andy's twenty-second birthday we had a party. I was not sure how many young people would show up, but to my surprise twenty-five of them came to our home. Not only that, they stayed until one o'clock in the morning talking about Andy. I furnished paper and pens for them to write comments to Andy, and a few of them did. We still have their notes. I realized too late some young people had not heard about Andy's memorial service and were hurt because they missed the funeral rite. This party gave them some closure and was therapeutic for them, as well as for Mike and me. We have never had another birthday party since but pleased we had the first one.

The second Thanksgiving my sister-in-law Judy had dinner at her home; a family custom prior to the death of Danny and Andy. I brought two religious candles to be lighted to represent Danny and Andy's presence. At home we keep a religious candle burning by Andy's picture as a symbol that his spirit is always present.

The second year of Andy's death, June 1996, Mike and I traveled to Europe and met Jean Charles with his fiancee, Helen, in Paris. Jean Charles lived with us in America for a year when he was fourteen and Andy was twelve. Jean Charles and Helen traveled through France with us and we visited churches along the way; at each church we offered candles in memory of Andy. Lighting a candle for Andy wherever we go has now become a custom for us. The lighting helps me feel Andy is with us in spirit.

Another gift came from the Donor Network, a letter regarding the recipients. In the process of donating Andy's organs the Donor Network asked us if we would like to learn about the recipients and receive any communications they might send. We immediately replied that we would like to hear about the people. A letter from the Donor Network was waiting for us when we returned from Washington in August 1994. The letter told us one woman in her forties with young children received one kidney, and a man in his forties in California received a kidney and Andy's liver. Two different people received cornea transplants and given sight, and an Arizona man in his forties with two children received Andy's heart. We were comforted that others could benefit from our loss.

A year later the Donor Network wrote and advised they had a letter for us from a recipient. They asked if we would like to have the letter. Once again we responded 'yes'. The Network is strict about confidentiality for the donor and the recipient, and all communications must go through the Donor Network. The letter was from the woman who had received one of Andy's kidneys. She had suffered kidney problems in her youth and had received her brother's kidney years before, but her body had rejected the transplant. She was on dialysis several times a day, and had a dialysis machine in her home when she received Andy's kidney. Her body had accepted Andy's kidney, and she was doing extremely well. The period for rejection was over, and the prognosis good. She wrote telling us of her gratitude and about her family. We responded and she has written once more.

Two years after Andy's death we heard from Donor Network again. The man who received Andy's heart had written a letter to us. Did we want the letter? Our reply was 'yes' and the letter was forwarded to our home. In the letter the man asked if we could meet. Through the Network we gave approval for the man to have our name and telephone number. As soon as he had our telephone number he called. His name is Herman and he lives in Chino Valley, Arizona, with his wife and two teenage sons. He asked if they could drive to Phoenix and meet us. We said 'yes' and made arrangements for them to visit on a Sunday afternoon. We were not sure what we had let ourselves in for, but eagerly awaited their arrival. Herman and his family were so eager to meet us they arrived in Phoenix several hours ahead of the scheduled time. Herman telephoned to ask if they could come early, our answer was to say 'of course'. The family arrived at our home: Herman, his wife Sharon, and their two sons, John fourteen, Matt twelve, and Smoky the family poodle.

The meeting was very emotional, but wonderful. The family, originally from West Virginia, moved to Arizona in 1992 for Herman's health. A doctor in West Virginia had told him he had rheumatoid arthritis. After the family arrived in Arizona, the doctors at the University of Arizona discovered he had a heart condition. Herman is a veteran of the Vietnam War, and there is speculation that he contracted a virus while in Vietnam that attacked his heart, destroying the organ.

Herman's condition was so critical that the doctors at Tucson Medical Center were preparing to insert an artificial heart when Andy's heart became available. Within twenty-four hours after receiving Andy's heart, Herman was up and walking around and requesting food. He had been living for the past five years near death, and he and his family were extremely grateful to us for having the compassion to donate Andy's heart. They are a warm caring family and Mike and I have come to love them. In his youth Herman was a lovable rascal like Andy and we could see Andy in his behavior. On one visit to Chino Valley to see the family, Herman was doing wheelies on an ATC, while

Mike and I looked at each other and laughed. That was something Andy would have been doing. John and Matt came to spend a week with us the first summer we met them, and we had a wonderful time. Our home is very quiet without young people around, and the boys filled the house with their presence. The family is very religious, and the sons have been raised well. Having faced the possible loss of their father, the boys are mature for their age, and very loving to their parents. We see the family several times a year and wish the visits could be more often.

August 4, 1998 was the fourth year of survival without Andy. Survival is the right word to define our lives. We are not really living yet, only surviving. At least surviving is all I have done. I do not presume to speak for Mike. Maybe next year, following the completion of this manuscript, faith will take me to the next phase in life without Andy. I can only hope and pray.

> *"He had a beautiful smile,*
> *an infectious laugh.*
> *To know him was to love him.*
> *He asked so little, and gave so much.*
> *Why did he have to go, we'll never know.*
> *He is our blithe spirit, forever with us.*
> *We miss him so, but in our heart we know,*
> *He is resting in God's arms forevermore."*

JG

Reflections

In the years following Andy's death, the question of "Why?" has always been present in my mind. I have found no answers to the why, only more questions. Looking back there are many decisions that could have been made differently, but given Andy's emotional vulnerability, I am not sure the outcome would have been different. Andy's perception of situations was always dramatic and negative. For example, some of the things he would say, in a given situation, would show a complete distortion of reality. Mike nor I ever considered or discussed moving Andy out of his and our home. Andy thought Mike's family did not like him, because they never paid any attention to him. The truth is, that when Mike's family gathers, they are simply happy to see one another and are busy talking and visiting among themselves.

In some of Andy's early drawings there are guns and fighting and death. To me the pictures were simply a typical boy's imagination of good guys versus bad guys. My intuition suggests the drawings were completely innocent. As a therapist, I am cautious about a professional tendency to see pictures of aggressive behavior as pathological. I can only guess Andy's negative thoughts the night he received the drunk-driving ticket. His wild imagination would see him losing his license, his job, and being kicked out of his home. None of those things would have been a reality.

After Andy died we received in the mail a two-month suspension of his driver's license; with permission to drive to and from work. Therefore, his job was secure. Mike and I would have been angry with Andy, yet we would have hired an attorney and paid the court costs to fight the citation. Throwing him out of the house would not have been an option. My thinking is that we would have insisted that he attend counseling and would have tried to have a doctor prescribe antidepressant medication for him. I know we would have pursued this action because we were already planning to persuade him to see a medical doctor for his condition. I was simply waiting for an opportunity to approach Andy about my decision; the drunk driving citation would have been perfect leverage for me to suggest he seek help. Would any of this have helped? We will never know.

Again, on reflection, so many coincidences seemed to be leading to his death, any one of which if altered could have saved his life. Andy was only three blocks from his home and safety when the police officer stopped him at 1:30 a.m. on the DUI charge. The officer saw the gun on the Mustang's dashboard. If the policeman had been more cautious he would have confiscated the gun. Maybe the law would not have allowed him to take the gun, but a gun in the hands of a drunk person is a dangerous situation.

The officer could have considered his condition as an excuse to take the gun. If he had retained him at the precinct office longer, giving him more time to recover, maybe he would not have killed himself. When I telephoned the police station following Andy's death the arresting officer was very hesitant about giving me information, I suspected the reason was fear of a lawsuit. I was not looking for someone to blame, but simply wanted to talk to the last person who had spoken with Andy. After the officer realized I just needed to talk about Andy, he told me he saw the gun on the dashboard of the Mustang, but had no legal authority to confiscate the firearm. The officer also explained that if there were no outstanding warrants the police do not retain a person overnight for drunk driving. I thought they did keep the offender overnight. Certainly, if he had spent the night in jail, he might have lived longer by having the time to resolve the issues. However, I am not sure the shame of spending a night in jail would not have made him kill himself anyway. Andy did have a certain pride about himself which spending a night in jail probably would have crushed.

The police officer also told me Andy was very pleasant and cooperative during the traffic stop. Andy told the officer he was upset about a recent breakup with his girl friend, but the officer said he did not seem depressed. How would the officer know, or would he even care? Perhaps police officers should have more training in psychology, they often deal with people who are psychologically disturbed at the time of an arrest.

I was awake at 1: 30 a.m., the time Andy was arrested, prowling around the house worrying about him. I went to the Arizona room to see if he was there. The room was dark, and empty. I returned to bed, but did not close the bedroom door completely, thinking I would hear him when he walked past the door of my room. I did have a pillow over my head, a habit developed to help drown out the noise when Andy was in the Arizona room with his friends. I am a very light sleeper and the slightest noise awakens me. Mike and Andy laughed about my sleeping with a pillow over my head, but I used the pillow anyway. Andy must have walked right by my partially open door to go to his room. Why did I not hear him? I was dozing lightly, and was half awake when I heard the gunshot. Andy had a second set of keys to the car in his room. I had planned to take the second set and keep the keys for him so they would not get lost, but, obviously forgot to put the second set away. If I had remembered, he would not have been able to retrieve his car which was parked three blocks away, with the gun still sitting on the dashboard. Andy would have had to wake me to get the other set of car keys; then I could have talked with him.

The house pets, Fuzzy and Gage, were sleeping on his bed where they always slept and he must have seen them. Why did he fail to stop and wake them up? The pets never made a sound when he entered the house; not even when the gun was fired or the paramedics arrived. Tim later asked why Andy had not called him. I had no answer. We do know he called his girl friend Kim because he left a message on her answering machine simply saying he had called to say goodbye. If Kim had been home and talked with Andy, would he still be alive? I very much doubt talking to her would have prevented his suicide, possibly only delayed the event.

My feeling is that Andy decided he wanted to die around his twenty-first birthday. He was disappointed when no one celebrated the big event and he was discouraged at the direction his life was going. Andy knew his father and I were disappointed in his choices. We kept telling him he could be and do anything he wanted. He was intelligent, good-looking, and had a wonderful personality. We had tried to get him to read a book the previous year called *Choices* by Shad Helmstetter. The story tells us we are in control of our lives. We make choices, good or bad, that affect whether we will be happy and successful or miserable and poor. The theory of *Choices* makes sense and Mike and I encouraged Andy to read the book. He never found the time. I look at pictures of Andy in happier days, and his eyes twinkle with the joy of living. In the month before he died, the light was gone from his eyes. His lips smiled, but his eyes were flat, and no person or event brought back the sparkle. I had helped him buy a newer car for his birthday, another Ford Mustang, yet he was not excited about his new car.

As Andy's confusion continued to develop, I was so overwhelmed with his pain I did not know what course to take. I was trying to be firmer with him, talking with him about being financially responsible and the necessity of taking control of his life. He was working as a courier for a law firm and beginning to carry his own weight financially.

His father was trying to be responsive to him, but could not see past the dollars Andy went through so casually. Mike had always worked hard for his money and was very conservative with spending. Andy was a spendthrift. He could not hang on to money and always seemed to need help financially. Mike could not relate to his behavior. Mike had been working since he was twelve years old, and his sense of values was completely different. On the other hand I do not care much about money. Money offers me security, and I spend conservatively but part with money easily, especially if someone needs assistance. My thinking is that Andy was disappointed in himself, but felt powerless to change his circumstances. He always looked at things in a negative way, which is typical of people who suffer from depression.

Cognitive therapy believes a person's way of thinking about a situation can be changed by looking at the problem from a more positive perspective. Probably, cognitive therapy works for some people, for some problems, sometimes. My personal experience with depression as a biochemical imbalance is that a person can think all the positive thoughts they want, but nothing will help their disposition. This is also because of the physical nature of the disorder. I have tried numerous techniques to overcome my depression and none of them have produced a lasting relief. For me the depression would come and go, being worse a week before my menstrual cycle. Sometimes I could feel the change in my brain chemistry as the change was occurring; one minute thinking negative thoughts and the very next minute thinking what a beautiful world in which we live. If cognitive therapy was the answer for depression, the thousands of people who suffer from depression would be relieved. Instead, many people who suffer from depression are still unable to change their thinking process due to the chemical imbalance in the brain.

There are many different kinds of antidepressant medicines on the market and they bring relief to some people. Some, like myself, have limited results. The only solution that has really helped my depression is physical activity. I must be physically active, and be able to exercise or the depression settles on me like a dark cloud. Even when I do not feel like exercising I force myself. I am a very self-disciplined person, and refer to my efforts as 'pulling myself up by the scruff of the neck'. I have always been physically active, describing myself as a 'doer' not a 'watcher'.

About twenty years ago I discovered being physically active helps me feel better when depressed. My exercises were walking and playing racquetball. As I became older I switched from racquetball to tennis, and walked on the days when not playing tennis. Hopefully, I will never have to stop playing tennis although arthritis in my hands is making holding the racquet difficult. I tried to get Andy involved with physical activities, but nothing he tried ever captured his interest. The only physical activities he ever enjoyed were going out into the desert and having paint gun wars, and driving a car, if driving can be considered a physical activity. When Andy was small he did like to go fishing; however, his father was not a fisherman and Andy soon lost interest. Andy liked Tae Kwon Do, but did not like the discipline involved in developing the skill. His involvement in the martial arts was very sporadic.

In retrospect, perhaps if Andy had been parented differently he would have had a better chance of surviving and dealing with his depression. My belief is that Mike and I did the best we knew how, but unfortunately, that best was not the best for Andy. Love was never an issue. He knew we loved him very much. I thought by loving him unconditionally that love would be enough, but love is never enough. A parent must give the child the tools with which to survive. A child needs unconditional love with daily 'living' boundaries established through reason and thought. Encouragement in accepting responsibility for one's actions and the consequences, is important for self-confidence and self-esteem.

Communication within the family is one area in which Mike and I neglected Andy. Mike is quiet and reserved. My style of communication was very passive-aggressive, meaning I would contain my feelings until I exploded. We never modeled effective communication for Andy, and so he never learned to express his own feelings. Andy and I talked and he could tell me anything, but he apparently thought he should be strong and silent like his father. When he became a teenager, he withdrew more into himself and did not communicate with us. When I would ask what was wrong he would tell me he did not want to talk about whatever was bothering him.

As Andy grew older I continued to try to talk to him when things were bothering him, but he would be very resistant to discussion. A pattern of my forcing him to sit and talk to me was established. At first he would be defensive and angry, and then he would calm down and we could talk. As Andy became an adolescent he was never able to talk with his father. Maybe if we had given him a better foundation on how to communicate he would have had better coping skills to deal with his depression and negative thought patterns. I have read many cases of young people committing suicide since Andy's death. Many of those youths did appear to feel good about themselves and did have better parenting, and yet even they were unable to overcome the desire to end their lives. This is why I am not sure even if Mike and I had been better parents Andy would be alive today.

Do some people come into this world with a predisposition toward self-destruction? If so, perhaps their paths cannot be altered. I can only guess and wonder. As a family counselor I have seen many young people who have had horrible parents and childhoods and never wanted to kill themselves. So, why are they still alive and our Andy is dead? I am not even sure which is more pathological, the desire to die or the desire to live. People cling to the most miserable existence in the world, and yet the individual continues to want to live. Other people who have every advantage find life unbearable. Myself, I find living in this world very difficult, because there is such pain and suffering. For example, young women sexually active and having babies by young men they eventually end up not even liking. I see newborn babies left in the trash, and child abuse that would give a civilized person nightmares. I see wonderful people suffer, and evil people prosper, and I know one thing: life is not fair.

We are teaching our children a lie when we tell them life will reward them if they pursue a specific pattern of behavior. No wonder some young people turn away from religion when their parents use religion to force them to behave in a manner the parents think is correct. God is not Santa Claus and He will not answer prayers just because we pray the right way or belong to the right church. Simply because a person's prayers are not answered does not mean that God loves them less, God loves us all unconditionally; and His heart breaks each and every time we suffer.

I agree with author Harold Kushner who writes that when God gave human beings free will this freedom included God not interfering even when we behave in a manner that will harm us. I do not believe God wanted my son to kill himself to teach Mike and me a lesson. The choice Mike and I have now, with the grace of God, is to attain whatever good we can from Andy's tragic and senseless death. This, I believe, is God's purpose. Every day I pray for the strength and courage to survive and to help others in whatever way I can.

I do not have answers to all the questions about death and particularly death by suicide, nor do the medical experts. The professionals can only hypothesize, so I guess I can hypothesize too. I think Andy wanted to live, but his sensitivity and negative perspective of things distorted his view of reality. For him, the drunk driving charge was the straw that broke the camel's back and brought him to the breaking point. Andy was in pain, and the alcohol in his system altered his thinking enough to allow him to kill himself. If he had been sober, perhaps he would not have killed himself; but I do think he was looking for an excuse to kill himself.

The words 'alcohol related death' make the death sound like alcohol was the cause. In truth, in the case of suicide, my professional experience is that the person is already intent on killing themselves. The alcohol simply numbs the person enough to allow them to complete the act. I do agree with the professionals that say when a person feels hopeless and helpless, there may not be any choice but to end the pain through death. A popular saying is that suicide is 'a permanent solution to a temporary problem'. I am not sure I agree the problem is temporary. Ask anyone who has lived with depression for a length of time and that person will tell you the dark way they feel is anything but temporary.

Recently, several students in my psychology class said they thought suicide is a selfish, cowardly act. In many ways this opinion is true. The person committing suicide is thinking only of themselves and their pain. They are certainly not thinking of the devastation their death will cause those who love them. The cowardly part goes with the fact life is difficult for everyone, but we all have the responsibility to endure together.

When a person commits suicide, they have left the rest of us alone to endure without them and that is not fair. Enduring this vale of tears called life is an unspoken covenant people have with one another. If a loved one chooses death willingly the rest of us feel cheated and angry, partly because we are left to survive without them. I have heard others say committing suicide takes courage, especially to put a gun to your head and pull the trigger; the courage to say 'I have had enough of the pain of this world and I want out'; the courage to say 'this is my life and I will live or die as I choose, not as society dictates'.

Our society rails at the idea someone has the right to take their own life, even if they are terminally ill and will die an excruciating death. Our American society believes any form of life, no matter how miserable is better than death. My belief is that our fear of death is based on a lack of faith that God does exist and there is a better life after death. What if God really is a hoax, and this life is all we have? Better this miserable existence than to cease to exist completely. Andy may have thought he was doing Mike and me a favor by ending his life. By dying he would not cost us more money and we could get on with our lives. On the other hand, he probably did not think of us at all. I do not believe he killed himself to 'show us' or 'get even'. Andy was too loving a person to deliberately inflict the kind of pain his death caused us and his friends. Perhaps, he really did believe he was doing everyone, including himself, a favor.

I do know Andy should be alive. His spirit lives in the hearts and minds of his father and me and many of his friends, but the spirit is different from a warm, breathing, laughing body. I will grieve for him until the day I die, as will his father. I have read books by psychics and even went to see a psychic a year ago. My need was to talk to someone about Andy, and if possible allow me to speak to him. I needed to hear that he forgave me for failing him. The medium was interesting, but not enlightening. I never believed in psychics and doubted the stories people told me.

My sisters-in-law recommended a female psychic who was reputed to be very effective in communicating with the deceased. I decided to visit this psychic and made an appointment to see her. I was very skeptical, and during the reading gave her no information about myself. She gives a person a life review and is not a medium who speaks through spirits. She made some comments that were comforting, but her predictions regarding my future were completely wrong. She has the dubious distinction of being100 percent incorrect on predicting future events for my life. So much for psychics. I do believe Andy's spirit is alive and dwelling in our home. His presence is why we want to stay in this house where he grew up, playing, and dying. I have experienced only a few dreams where Andy has come to me and I could smell him and feel the warmth of his body as he hugged me.

My first dream occurred several years after Andy died. In the dream Andy was naked as the day he was born, and came running toward me calling "Mommy, Mommy." He was about two years old, and jumped into my arms, smelling that wonderful baby powder smell after having just taken a bath. I could see him, smell him, hear his voice and feel his sweet warm body in my arms. The dream gave me so much peace and comfort. A year or so later, while in church thinking of him, suddenly I felt his presence next to me. He was taller than me and had to lean down to place his arm across my shoulders. He gave me a hug and whispered, "I love you." Unfortunately, these wonderful experiences of his presence have been far too few.

Sometimes, my heart tells me Andy's death was for the best; he was probably going to have a very difficult life. His inability to make wise choices was a pattern familiar to many people, young and old. Typically, the person continues to make wrong choices in career, mates and life, never being able to understand why situations never seem to work for their benefit. Now he is saved the pain that goes with living and taking chances.

On the other hand, my thinking is that Andy would have eventually gotten his life on track and been happy and successful at whatever he chose to do. Andy's core was solid. He was kind and gentle and compassionate. He had the strength of his convictions and was an honorable young man. Andy was never rude to adults, treating them with respect. Everyone liked Andy, except those who 'ran into his wrong side'. Possibly, if he had been fortunate enough to have had his first love relationship work, he might have taken a different road. I do not think the possibility of his love being rejected ever occurred to him, and when his love was spurned the disappointment destroyed his self-esteem. In my opinion, first love often sets a pattern for a person's attitude toward love and future relationships. He should be here with me learning to walk through the pain of life and growing from his mistakes. He should have lived to be married and have children. He should have been the one to bury us, but we had to bury him. He cheated us and himself of the opportunity to develop into the kind of man God always intended him to be.

On the other hand, Andy gave us many gifts through his death. For his friends, he taught them what a true friend is, and through his death they came to realize the meaning of friendship. For Mike and me, Andy's death has made us appreciate the short time we had with him. His death has also given us a greater love for one another than we had before. With that love is a new appreciation for the positive qualities and strengths each has to offer. I now truly appreciate Mike's quiet commitment to me and our marriage. My admiration for Mike continues to grow. He is the most honorable man I know, and I respect him more than any man I have met.

Mike has told me and his friends that I am the 'world's greatest lover'. By this comment he means I am kind and loving to everyone, no matter who they are. I accept people as they are, not as I would have them be, and give without asking or expecting anything in return. Mike has teased me about the misfits and the lost people I tend to draw around me. Now he accepts the fact that I simply like helping people. I always give to street people, who am I to judge what they do with the money. They are entitled to live their lives as they choose; if I am a sucker, 'so be it'. Giving a dollar here and there does not hurt me, and the dollar may help them find food or lodging or comfort.

Another gift Andy has given us is the desire to live life now, and not wait until we are old and retired. We travel and pursue interests now instead of waiting until later. We have gone to

England and France where we saw our former exchange student, Jean Charles and his fiancee. We have hiked part of St. James Pilgrimage, which is in the northern part of Spain. On another vacation we spent a wonderful time with friends on a yacht in the British Virgin Islands. Mike, who was always too busy working, is now eager to travel and experience new adventures. I was always ready to travel before Andy's death, but we did not have the time or the money. Now Mike is the one who is ready for adventure. For me, some of the challenge of life is less interesting.

Mike is all I have left of Andy, and I think Mike sees me in the same way. We love each other, and our love for Andy makes our love for each other even stronger. These emotions are gifts Andy has left for us. Another of his gifts to us is his many friends who honor Mike and me by wanting us to be a small part of their lives. These young people have parents, yet they take the time to stop by, or call and invite us to their graduation, wedding, or to see their new baby. Herman, the man who has Andy's heart, is a loving part of our life. His sons, John and Matt, love us for the gift of life we gave their father. They are wonderful young men, and we hope always to be a part of their lives. In so many ways Mike and I are truly blessed, and yet would give up these wonderful blessings to have our beloved son. These gifts are poor substitutes for our child, but are better than nothing at all, and do help to ease the pain.

Where I go from here is a question I have been struggling with since Andy died. The life I was living when Andy was alive is gone, ashes, like my Andy; like the mythical bird, the Phoenix, how do I rise from the ashes? One well-meaning friend said God had given me this burden so that I could help other survivors of suicide. People say many well-meaning but stupid words when trying to comfort someone who has lost a loved one. At the time following Andy's death I had neither the strength nor the desire to walk through this kind of pain with others who suffer the loss of a loved one through suicide. Now maybe I am ready, with the help of God, to begin the fight against the ignorance and shame involved in suicide. I have been appalled during these past years to find so little information about suicide. Much of the information available showed me how little we know or understand suicide.

The myths about suicide that existed when I was a youth are the same myths that exist today. Young people constantly tell me that people who talk about suicide are simply trying to get attention, and will not really commit the act. How very wrong they are. When Andy was sixteen, his friends knew he had held a gun to his head, yet told no adult about the act, or worried that Andy might repeat the threat. I do not blame the boys for their ignorance, but I am saddened. I might have sought professional help for Andy earlier if I had known of his behavior. I have a sister-in-law whose son suffered from depression and was on medication, but Mike and I never knew. The parents may have been embarrassed, or simply protecting their son's confidentiality, but the information might have helped me show Mike that Andy needed help. I cite these cases not to make anyone feel guilty or responsible, but to illustrate the consequences of depression among young people.

My prayer is that this manuscript will inspire some hearts and therefore some people into action to prevent more senseless loss of life. I want to spend the rest of my life sharing my loss with people in the hope of educating them about the reality of depression and suicide. Telling others of my loss and my shame is not easy. If I can save one person the pain of loss each time I share my story, then my heartache will be worth the cost. My hope is that medical professionals and family oriented organizations will implement programs educating young people, and adults, about the tragedy of suicide: before, not after an individual commits suicide. Taking the shame and the secrecy out of suicide through educating society will allow survivors to hold their heads up, and admit their loved one committed suicide. There are few support groups for survivors of suicide.

As far as I am aware we have no support groups for *preventing* suicide. When asked, many people admit having thought at one time or another of ending their life, and yet were able to survive the thought. If there were not so much shame in admitting thoughts of suicide, maybe fewer people would kill themselves. By admitting they were considering suicide, individuals could receive support and survive the feeling. I am suggesting that by sharing my shame and loss that this sharing will bring suicide out of the closet; and do for suicide prevention what Mothers Against Drunk Driving (MADD) has done to get drunks off the road. By this statement I do not mean passing a law making suicide illegal; suicide is already illegal, the law simply has not been ridiculous enough to arrest a dead person for killing themselves. I am suggesting help could be given to potential victims of suicide by funding money for education and awareness, for community support groups, and professional therapy.

> *"Therefore we pray to You instead, O God,*
> *for strength, determination, and willpower,*
> *to do instead of just pray,*
> *to become instead of merely to wish."*

> *Likrat Shabbat*
> *Jack Riemer*

Epilogue

The fifth-year anniversary of Andy's death was August 4, 1999. Looking back, I wonder where the time has gone and how the world continues to exist. I am constantly reminded of the things Andy is missing in life. Recently, Mike and I were given the honor of being Eucharistic ministers at the wedding of a friend of Andy's. Jason is one of his dear friends who has stayed in touch with us since the death. He, too, has struggled to accept and understand Andy's senseless death.

At the wedding party, I saw Andy's three closest friends from elementary school. He would have been a part of the wedding if he were alive. He was present in spirit as his father and I 'stood in' for him. Richard, probably Andy's dearest friend in elementary school, was Jason's best man. Tim was an usher, and I am sure Andy would have been an usher as well. These three young men have grown up to be kind and caring individuals. Seeing them allows me to see what Andy could have been, as they choose their careers and wives. Richard married his sweetheart in Maryland in October 1997. Jason married in May 1998, and Tim is planning to marry in the near future. Jason and Tim's parents felt that our presence as Eucharistic ministers was a fitting honor to Andy. Watching Jason and his bride's ceremony in Brophy Chapel, where we attended mass for so many years, was very painful.

As I write this epilogue at 1:00 o'clock in the morning I realize God did answer our prayers for Andy, although not the way Mike and I had planned. Mike always prayed Andy would be a man of God, and I always wanted Andy to be happy. I think both of those prayers have been answered. He is with God now, and he is sharing in the peace and joy of being with our Father. There are those who think people who commit suicide are sinners, and will be denied God's love. I disagree.

My belief is that hell is here on earth, and when we die, we go to a much better place. A place where we share the peace and joy we never experienced on earth. I know Andy's spirit attended Jason's wedding with us and he experienced joy in seeing his friends together and happy. As I hugged each of these three young men at the wedding, the love they have for Andy shone in their faces. The four boys are very different personalities, but they shared their youth together and enjoyed each other's company. Jason and Richard the more serious ones, Tim and Andy fun loving. I believe Andy will live in the hearts of these three young men forever.

Writing this manuscript has been the most difficult and painful task I have experienced since Andy's death. I knew the process of reliving the past years would be difficult, but felt the writing of this story was a commitment I had to accomplish. In therapy, the psychological word 'catharsis' is often used; i.e., the purging of the spirit. Catharsis is an appropriate term to use in referring to the writing of this manuscript. The process has been a purging for me, a challenge I hope will allow me to let go of my sense of guilt and shame of having failed as a mother. My prayer is that this process will allow me to help others by bringing the mystery and myths about suicide into the open. I have also learned a great deal about suicide in the process.

In the beginning, I did not know much about suicide and the limited information available to the public. When I have been willing to share my loss with others, people in response have often told me of a loss of someone through suicide; or their own fear for a loved one suffering from depression. By opening the door for discussion about suicide perhaps others will be allowed to ask questions and express their concerns about death. Many people are very uncomfortable when they learn your child committed suicide. They look at you in a way that suggests you must have been a horrible parent. I have found out who my friends are during this time, and have been surprised by those who have drifted away because of being uncomfortable around Mike and me. My feeling is of sadness for them, but I understand.

Mike and I have to move forward; we cannot stay in the past. As we move forward our true friends and family, along with new friends we make along the way, support and encourage us as we struggle on without our son. Our lives are forever changed. In this life, we will always miss our beloved son, but we will be trying to make the best of what the rest of our time has to offer.

My tennis helps me maintain my sanity, and Mike has the ranch. I play tennis two or three times a week, and Mike rides his horse every weekend during the Spring and Fall roundups at the ranch near Yarnell. The ranch is like stepping back in time. At the end of the day the riders sit around the dinner table. No one watches television or listens to the radio. Being in the countryside, riding and performing physical labor, is probably the greatest therapy for Mike. On the ranch, he can forget about the corporate world and concentrate on rounding up the cattle, branding, and sorting the animals for market. During roundups in April and October, Mike drives his truck to the ranch on Friday night, and returns late Sunday night; tired, dirty and refreshed in spirit. I have joined Mike at the ranch several times. Usually, there are about nine people who ride each weekend, and we go out in teams of two to search the range for cattle. I found the experience unbelievably peaceful and relaxing. I had no trouble sleeping at night after an eight-hour day in the saddle. In the mountains, the days are cooler than Phoenix and the night sky is brilliant with stars.

At the ranch we met an artist who does carvings and paintings. Mike and I commissioned him to make a wooden urn for Andy's ashes. He took a beautiful, natural piece of wood and created a vase, where we now keep Andy's ashes. The vase sits on his wooden high chair that I had lovingly stained and finished for my son so many years ago.

Andy's death gave many of his friends a wake-up call. His friends will never forget Andy and all he taught them about being a 'real' friend. His bright smile and wonderful laugh are just a few of the gifts he shared with us while he was here. Now we have wonderful memories and photographs to remind us of the good times we had together, and the joy he brought his father and me. Mike and I would trade these gifts for a second chance, but we know this wish is not possible. Instead, we thank God and Andy for the joy he gave us.

I hope my story may inspire enough compassion and understanding to help establish a foundation that would work toward the prevention of suicide by young people, through education and counseling. I have come to the conclusion through writing this manuscript that Andy's death was a sad waste of a special individual. Through his death many of us have had to examine our hearts and search for answers where there are none. Hopefully, we are better people than we were before his death. I know we are certainly different now than before. Now I have to find a new meaning and purpose for my life. To this end, I have turned control of my life over to God. I ask God to give me the strength, determination, and willpower to 'do' instead of just pray, to 'become' instead of merely wish to do God's will.

> *"God created me to do Him some definite service; He has committed some work to me which He has not committed to another. I have my mission. Therefore, I will trust Him."*
>
> *J. H. Newman*
> *The Newman Center*

"But people who pray for courage, for strength to bear the unbearable, for the grace to remember what they have left instead of what they have lost, very often find their prayers answered."

<u>When Bad Things Happen to Good People</u>
Harold Kushner

Acknowledgments

First of all, I want to thank God for carrying me through the most devastating period of my life. Without His love, I could not have survived the loss of my beloved son. Next, thanks to my dear husband for standing by me during this difficult time. His courage and ever abiding faith has inspired me and given me strength to survive these years. I want to thank Anna Corbett-Wall for guiding me through the stages of grief, and for being a friend as well as a counselor to me. Sincere thanks to Ralph Tanner, my publisher. Ralph's expertise and encouragement helped me transform a poorly written story into a readable and hopefully thought provoking manuscript. Ralph has become a friend as well as a mentor during the writing and editing of this manuscript, and I thank God for putting him in my life at just the right time. A special thanks to Bill Kornovich, Jan Holt, Ronda Parker, Larissa Spraker, and Karyl Fehlman for their editorial contributions.

A thank you also goes to Tonya Mock, Leza Lachapelle-Dandos, Pat Stone, Arnold Corella, John Lyons, and Richard Howe for the KUSK-TV (Prescott, AZ) television coverage. Their generosity and dedication in promoting adolescent suicide awareness is sincerely appreciated.

Thanks also goes to Judge Maurice Portley for giving so generously of his time, and to U. S. Surgeon General David Satcher for bringing attention to the problem of adolescent suicide in our country. And a thank you also goes to all my friends and family members who have believed in me and encouraged me to write Andy's story.

Joyce Gatson
May 2000

Appendices

Suicide Information Resources

1. American Association of Suicidology
    4201 Connecticut Avenue, NW, Suite 310
    Washington, DC 20008
    Phone: (202) 237-2280
    FAX: (202) 237-2282
    web site: www.cyberpsycho.org
    E-mail: berm101@ix.netcom.com

2. EMPACT - SPC
    1232 E. Broadway Road, Suite # 120
    Tempe, AZ 85282
    Office: (602) 784-1514
    Crisis Line: (602) 784-1500
    FAX: (602) 967-3528

3. The Compassionate Friends, Inc.
    (For bereaved parents)
    National Headquarters
    P. O. Box 3696
    Oak Brook, Illinois 60522-3696
    (708) 990-0010

Andy's Prayer

I was walking with the Lord one day, hand in hand, when the Lord said to me, "It is time to pick today's bouquet for me to carry." We walked toward this magnificent gate, that could be seen for as far as the eye could see. I heard these beautiful sounds of music that made me stop to listen. The Lord opened the gate and the sounds flooded the air all around. The butterflies were dancing over miles and miles of the most glorious flowers any eye could ever behold. I stared in awe. This was the most beautiful sight my eyes had ever seen. The birds were singing God's favorite hymns.

In the middle of all these beautiful flowers stood one little rose with his head drooping and tears on his face. The Lord said, "I will pick this one first today." As he lifted up the little rose I saw the name of Andy on its petals. I said, "Oh no Lord, not today! Can't you spare him to us a little longer?" The Lord replied, "Dear child, please don't question my way. You will understand someday." As He picked up the little rose in His loving hands, I saw this beautiful smile come upon the little rose's face. The Lord dried Andy's tears and held him tenderly. I saw the peace of the world in His loving hands.

Then my eyes opened and I saw mom and dad's loving faces,

and all the other loved ones who had gone ahead and I knew everything was going to be all right. I knew Andy had gone home and would be fine until we all joined him in that heavenly garden and I felt peace.

The Lord said, "Now it is time for you to go back and tell the others all is fine." As I left, I took one more look back. The little rose was smiling and waving in the breeze. I said, "Andy I will be back to see you one day." His reply was, "I will be waiting here for all of you."

He shouted to me, "Tell Mom and Dad it wasn't their fault; I just didn't belong, so I had to come home." When I looked into his big blue eyes, I knew he was right. He said, "Tell Mom and Dad I will be with them every day. They will feel my loving presence. They will hear my voice, close their eyes and see my face. Tell them I had to come home and take my place with the Lord. Tell them I'm sorry for hurting them. They were great. Mom and Dad, please forgive me."

"Remember above all others I loved you both dearly, and with all my heart."

Your loving son forever, Andy.

A message recalled from a dream about Andy by Aunt Ina, September 1994.

Jason's Dream

Jason had a dream about Andy a few months after Andy died. The dream frightened him so badly, he was afraid to go back to sleep. At the time of the dream, Jason was attending the University of Arizona in Tucson. The dream terrified him so badly, he decided to cut his classes and come home to Phoenix to talk with his mother and me about his dream.

Jason called me and made arrangements to come to our home and share his dream with me. In his dream he saw Andy's red Firebird. In the car was a girl. All Jason could see was the back of the girl's head, she had long blonde hair; then Jason saw Andy walking around the side of the car to greet him. Andy had a big smile on his face and seemed to be welcoming Jason. Andy also had a red gash on the left side of his face, on his cheek. Jason awakened, frightened and not sure what to make of the dream. For days after the dream Jason was afraid to go to sleep for fear of having the dream again, and what the dream might mean.

I explained to Jason that Andy's wound had been to his right temple, and not his left cheek. I assured him the dream was probably Andy's way of trying to reassure Jason that everything was all right and not to be so sad about his death.

Andy was not calling Jason to join him, but was there only to reassure Jason that going on with his life was what Andy wanted him to do.

I reassured Jason that he had every right to be angry with Andy, because Andy had done a stupid thing, and hurt many people by his actions. Andy probably never really meant to kill himself, but did not know how to live. I encouraged Jason to yell, scream and cuss at Andy for leaving him, and that Andy would understand. Also, I assured Jason that Andy would always be with him and celebrate in all of Jason's successes and comfort him in his disappointments.

Jason told me how much he missed Andy, that he could do things with Andy that no one else liked to do, and that without him these things were no longer fun. For example, he and Andy liked to simply sit outside under the stars at night and stare at the universe without saying a word. Other friends thought staring at the stars was a dumb pastime. Jason is such a quiet young man, I think Andy brought out the kid in him.

Jason told me he felt close to Andy whenever he came to visit at our home. Jason felt that our house was like a second home, and he always felt comfortable here. Jason, like Andy, said he did not really want to grow up and be an adult, he wanted to stay a kid like Andy. I wonder what we adults have done to make adulthood look so uninviting to our youth.

A few days later I spoke with Cecilia, Jason's mother. She too had a long talk with Jason and had comforted her eldest son, so that he fell asleep peacefully across his mother's bed for the first time since he had the dream of Andy. Cecilia, too, expressed her anger and sorrow at Andy for what he had done. I assured Cecilia that I was okay with her expressing her feelings, and that I understood how she felt.

In that same week Jason met with Andy's other dear friends,

Tim and Alin. The three of them came to the conclusion Andy had not really meant to kill himself, but was simply 'pushing the envelope', as Tim referred to Andy's reckless behavior.

The following week Jason called late one night. He was calling to thank us for having Andy. He said Andy was a wonderful kid and now Andy knew more than Jason. Jason said he always thought of Andy as dumb, but now Andy was smarter than he, because Andy now knows what death is. Somehow, Andy was able to fill whatever special needs each of his friends had.

Transcribed by Joyce Gatson

Aunt Ina's Vision

My sister, Ina, believes with all her heart that Andy saved her life the night he died. She and a friend were coming home about two o'clock in the morning, at the same time I saw Andy's spirit leaving his body. Ina and her friend were broadsided by a hit-and-run driver on a lonely mountain road in California. My sister, who has a heart condition, prayed to God to help them. Moments later a young man appeared in a pickup truck. He comforted my sister, and told her he would go for help, and then he would return to be with Ina and her friend until help arrived. The young man did return, but as soon as the paramedics arrived, he disappeared, and no trace of him or his being there was ever found. The paramedics claimed there was no one else but my sister and her friend at the site when they arrived. Another gift from Andy? We will never know for sure.

Joyce Gatson

Christmas 1994 Letter to Friends

God grant you the joy and peace of this holiday season.

Our grief is too great at this time for us to celebrate the

traditional holiday,

but we wish you all joy and happiness.

We want to thank all of you who have been there for us

during this difficult time. God gives us the promise that we

will be reunited with Andy on another day,

not so very far away,

and this is our hope.

May God grant you Peace,

Mike and Joyce Gatson

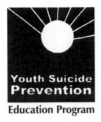

Youth Suicide
Prevention
Education Program

July 14, 2000

As a result of the preparation and research for this manuscript, and discussions with parents, teachers and clergy – and survivors of suicide – the decision was made to establish a national information/training program to prevent adolescent suicide and to assist the survivors.

The Youth Suicide Prevention Education Program was approved for incorporation by the Arizona Corporation Commission on December 13, 1999; the U.S. Internal Revenue Service granted a nonprofit status effective December 13, 1999.

This multidimensional program presents a forum for at risk young people; and an education and information center for parents, teachers, mental health professionals, legal advocates and clergy.

The U.S. Surgeon General, David Satcher, M.D., stated recently in a nationally televised program that "adolescent suicide is a national epidemic…"

The focus of Youth Suicide Prevention Education Program is to save one young life, somewhere.

Joyce Gaton

1432 E. San Juan   Phoenix, Arizona 85014
telephone: 602/279-7880   e-mail: jgatson@home.com